LETTERS TO PADRE PIO

Volume One

(July 20, 2011 - December 11, 2012)

I0168124

OREST STOCCO

LETTERS TO PADRE PIO

Copyright © 2013 by OREST STOCCO

ISBN 978-0-9879357-9-3

Edited by Penny Lynn Cates

Cover Design by Penny Lynn Cates

"I can be of more use to you in heaven than I have been on earth. I belong to everyone; everyone will say Padre Pio is mine. I can refuse no one, since the Good Lord has never refused my humble requests."

PADRE PIO: THE TRUE STORY
C. Bernard Ruffin

"The modern man is not eager to know in what way he can imitate Christ, but in what way he can live his own individual life, however meager and uninteresting he may be. He may not know it, but he behaves as if his own individual life were instinct with the will of God, which must at all costs be fulfilled."

MODERN MAN IN SEARCH OF A SOUL
C. G. Jung

FOREWORD

Padre Pio is a modern day Roman Catholic Saint. He was born on May 25, 1887, died on September 23, 1968, and Pope John Paul II canonized him on June 16, 2002. He is known throughout the world as the Healing Saint because so many miracles have been attributed to him. I can attest to the miracle of his sanctifying grace, which I've written about in my novel Healing with Padre Pio that was inspired by a series of monthly spiritual healing sessions that I had with a very gifted spiritual sensitive who channeled St. Padre Pio for me from the months of August 2010 to June 2011.

Of course, there will be those that will doubt it was St. Padre Pio that came through in my spiritual healing sessions, but I know that this venerable Saint of Humility, as I came to call him, slew my vanity and gave me a spiritual healing, and I have absolutely no doubt that it was the same humble Capuchin monk Francesco Forgione from Pietrelcina, Italy who became the "man of hope and prayer" and Ascended Spiritual Master St. Padre Pio.

You see, I was a very angry Roman Catholic who left the Church and needed a Roman Catholic Saint to heal my anger at Christianity; that's why Providence introduced me to St. Padre Pio, because only a Saint who had suffered the wounds of Jesus Christ could understand the wounds that the Roman Catholic Church had inflicted upon my soul.

I was young when I left the Church. I could not suffer the claustrophobia of my rigid faith and had to find the freedom that I hungered for, so I became a spiritual seeker. I found the teaching of reincarnation, which introduced me to the perennial philosophy of life, known simply as the Way; and I pursued the Way wherever my search took me.

Strangely enough, after years of searching the Way brought me right back to the teachings of Jesus, the "strait gate" of the "narrow way," ("Strait is the gate and narrow is the way, which leadeth unto life, and few there be that find it," Math. 7: 14), which I saw in a different light now; and I lived the "narrow way" of Christ for years until I found the spiritual path best suited to my new state of consciousness.

My new path was the Way of the Eternal, which I have lived for over thirty years now; but I came to a spiritual impasse in my path that I could not break through, and Providence saw fit to introduce me to St. Padre Pio who was channeled by the sensitive who gave me a complimentary spiritual healing at her open house. I pursued my spiritual healing with her and wrote a novel called *Healing with Padre Pio*; and now I'm writing St. Padre Pio a series of letters that he would like me to share with the world.

Bear in mind however that I'm not writing these letters from the perspective of a Roman Catholic to a Catholic Saint, but as a former Catholic who has his own spiritual view on life born of my life-long quest for answers to the questions: where do we come from? Who are we? And, where are we going? And I'm not writing them to a Roman Catholic Saint as such, but to an Ascended Spiritual Master who revealed to me that he has the consciousness of all knowing and all seeing.

When I asked him in my last spiritual healing session if he would like to work with me on another book because I enjoyed our relationship for my novel *Healing with Padre Pio*, he replied, "Our work is not yet done, my son."

Our work is bridging the two opposing worldviews that impede the flow of the River of God: Christianity's worldview that made Padre Pio an Ascended Spiritual Master—the dogmatic belief in one life and one savior; and the gnostic worldview of the Way that awakened me to my higher self.

I invite you to join me in my epistolary journey with Padre Pio, the venerable Saint of Humility whose spiritual wisdom transcends Christianity and embraces the whole world. He is truly a wonderful traveling companion.

Orest Stocco,
Bluewater, Georgian Bay
Tuesday, July 19, 2011

TABLE OF CONTENTS

ADDENDUM

INSIGHTS: A Timeless Wisdom
THE MAKING OF A NOVEL: *Jesus Wears Dockers, The Gospel Conspiracy Story*
AN INTERVIEW WITH THE AUTHOR: Open questions at a reading of *Healing with Padre Pio*

1. AT YOUR BEHEST

Letters to Ascended Master
St. Padre Pio,
Wednesday, July 20, 2011
3: 40 P.M.

Dear Padre,

I was sitting on our front deck waiting for Penny to come home from work this afternoon (I had just made a vegetarian pizza ready for the oven when she pulled into the yard) reading the new spiritual musing I had just written when the thought came to me—and very strongly, I might add, which led me to suspect that it was you who inspired it—to write you a book of letters.

Since I've always wanted to write a book of letters, I relished the idea of writing to an Ascended Spiritual Master, especially since we've already established a relationship with my novel *Healing with Padre Pio*. True, our relationship is couched in fiction, which I had to do for a variety of reasons; but that doesn't negate the reality of our experience. For me, you were very real when my spiritual sensitive channeled you; but this is different, because letter writing opens a window onto one's soul in an entirely different way.

Letter writing doesn't give one the latitude of fiction, but it is so much more intimate and personal, which is what I want this book of letters to be; something like your letters to your Spiritual Directors (*Secrets Of A Soul*), which I loved reading because you were so revealing and so on fire with the Holy Flame of God, but I would like my letters to be more in the spirit of someone who has found his own way back home to God and would like to share his journey with an Ascended Master who now serves life from the Other Side.

I have no set agenda with this project, other than that writing you will fuel the Holy Flame of God in my life—because it's to the nature of the creative spirit to set one's soul ablaze with inspiration; so I don't know where this is going to take me. It may not go anywhere, but the thought alone is enough to fill my heart with new wonder, because I know from our last project how you worked your miracles in my life. I know that this book of private letters will also find its own way; and I know that it will attract its own material just as all my books do, and I look forward to the surprises.

I should mention in this, my first letter to you, whom I consider to be more than a mere Catholic Saint (mere!), but an Ascended Spiritual Master, that my letters will be addressed to a Christian Saint who has transcended his Roman Catholic religion and speaks with a consciousness of all knowing and all seeing, as you revealed to me in one of my healing sessions; which means that I am free to speak my mind about the spiritual life with you regardless of your earthly religion, and mine—which as you well know happened to be Roman Catholicism also before I went on my quest for my true self.

I'm on a new spiritual path now, which I've been on for the past thirty-some years, and which I may reveal down the road; but for now, suffice to say that I have always taken my wisdom where I find it, and in you I have found a vein of pure spiritual gold!

So, with your blessing (I know that you've already given me the nod), I'm going to embark upon this project—if not for personal growth, for the rich literary experience that it will give me. You did say to me at the end of my spiritual healing sessions, "Our work is not yet done, my son." So, I'm rolling up my sleeves...

I remain your humble—I wrote the word "student," but no sooner did I write it and I felt you snatch the word away and replace it with the word "companion." "Spiritual companion," you insist. I'm comfortable with that, despite what some of my readers may think. Until the next time,

In Spirit,
Your fellow companion,
Orest

2. A MAN OF HOPE

Letters to Ascended Master
St. Padre Pio,
Thursday, July 21, 2011
9: 30 A. M.

Dear Padre,

Padre Pio, Man of Hope, by Renzo Allegri was my favorite of the ten books that I have read on your life so far, which I devoured with voracious curiosity after I met you through my spiritual sensitive, because I wanted to know everything about you; and although you were the same person that came through in the biographies of your life (and in your own letters and all the Padre Pio miracle stories, of which there were more than enough to choke an incredulous horse), you came through with the spiritual freedom of someone who had transcended the inflexible doctrine of your Roman Catholic religion—despite how you defended the false premises that I so vocally threw at you in my spiritual healing sessions as a challenge to the faith that you lived and died for.

But what I loved about how you defended the doctrine of your Roman Catholic faith (which was the bane of my youth), even though you knew that some of the tenets were false—like the doctrine of one life, for example; eternal damnation, and the forgiveness of sins, which I will bring up in other letters—was the way you managed to get me to shift my own inflexible perspective and appreciate the spiritual goodness of the religion that I turned on in one of my past lives that surfaced in my regressions five years ago.

Not that I didn't appreciate Christ's teaching, not at all; I would not have found my true self without Christ's teaching. It's what Christianity has done with Christ's teaching of the Way that I raged at. But let's not dwell on that today. I want to pay homage to you in this letter, because the more I heard what you had to say in my spiritual healing sessions, and the more I studied your life the more humbled I was by your unbelievable commitment to *la via di sofferenza*—the way of suffering.

You pleaded with your lord and savior to assist him in his mission, and Jesus invited you to participate in his passion by granting you the stigmata, the five wounds that he suffered during his crucifixion, which came to define your life. Renzo Allegri wrote: "he had endured incredibly enormous suffering, accusations, slanders, trials, and condemnations than one can imagine" (*Padre Pio, Man of Hope* p. 5), and the more I read about your life, the more I came to believe this—and that's when your passionate commitment to Jesus Christ's mission began to break through the walls of my own spiritual conceit and devastate the vanity that kept me from making further progress on my journey home to God!

"When people write about Padre Pio," wrote Renzo Allegri, "they tend to dwell on the penitential aspect of his life, thereby giving a somewhat dark and medieval tinge to his personality. But this is not really the case. Padre Pio was, and is a man of hope" (p. 6)

This is how you came through in my spiritual healing sessions—not dark and penitential (although, I felt shades of this quality in your character)—with a lightness of spiritual freedom and clarity that blew me away. I couldn't believe how contemporary and New Age you were in your spiritual perspective. In fact, I soon realized just how far ahead of the life curve you were, and this induced such excitement that I couldn't wait for my next spiritual healing session with you!

So, Padre; let me thank you in this letter for healing me of the vanity that kept me stuck in the River of God, because once your healing grace devastated my spiritual conceit I began to ride the currents to new and exciting possibilities—to the point, as you revealed, where I actually transcended my own voice and the voice of my spiritual community!

I wrote about this in *Healing with Padre Pio*; but I confess, I haven't written the last chapter yet ("The Vanity of All Spiritual Paths"). I have to let the manuscript sit and simmer for a few months before I read it through and bring my novel to closure. For now, I want you to know that I sense that this epistolary project has already begun to take form. Be it ever so subtle, the form is taking shape, and I know it won't be long before the dominant theme sprouts like a seed fully formed, and I can't wait to see what fruit it bears!

On a more personal note, I'd like to say that I have steeled myself to take on the household tasks that I've been putting off for—how long now, two, three, five years?—but I haven't quite gone that far yet to actually commit myself to do them. I do however feel that you have planted the thought of doing "one small household responsibility to begin with," which would begin breaking the hold that my little procrastinating self has on me; so I'll see what I can do.

I can't promise when, but I will entice myself by promising to not write you again until I do at least one household responsibility—*which should be interesting!*

I remain,
Your fellow companion,
Orest

3. AS PROVIDENCE WOULD HAVE IT

Letters to Ascended Master
St. Padre Pio,
Tuesday, July 25, 2011
6: 40 A. M.

Dear Padre,

I'm writing you a letter, so I must have granted myself permission by doing a household responsibility, which I did yesterday; I finally took my long extension ladder out and removed the dead branches from one of our maple trees that a severe storm last year had broken off, and I also cut four or five other dead branches from the tree. I want to remove the whole tree, which I may do in the fall with my neighbor Tony's help because he has a power saw, which will leave one large healthy maple and two small maples in that clump of trees in the center of our front yard. In any event, I see this as a symbolic sign—getting rid of the dead wood in my life!

Okay, now I can get to the reason I was dying to write to you about—the new book that I came across last week by "chance"!

As I said in my first letter, once I begin a new book it begins to attract to itself all the relevant material it needs to realize itself, and last week I drove into Barrie to visit my friend at her used bookstore and as Providence would have it I noticed a book on the coffee table where I was sitting that caught my attention— *In the Spirit of Happiness: Spiritual Wisdom for Living,* by the Monks of New Skete. (I will comment on this book in future letters, because it addresses much of what you had to say to me.)

My friend was busy placing an order of jewelry with a salesman (she sells more than used books in her New Age bookstore), so I went down the street to Tim Hortons and picked up a coffee for her, the salesman, and myself and sat down in one of her comfortable reading chairs to wait for her to finish her business; and while I waited I browsed the books that she had on the coffee table. One was *In the Spirit of Happiness*.

New Skete is an Orthodox Catholic monastery in Cambridge, New York, and as I read the inside cover jacket I was immediately pulled into the book because it excited my curiosity about the monastic life. I had not read any books on the monastic life until I began reading about your life, and for some reason Providence deemed it necessary for me to become acquainted with the spiritual life of a Catholic monastic order; hence my "discovery" of *In the Spirit of Happiness*, by the Monks of New Skete.

I had read a book called *Hermits,* by Peter Francis—with chapters on "The Desert Fathers," "By Walden Pond: Henry David Thoreau," "Hermit of the Sahara: Charles Foucauld," "The Waters of Contradiction: Thomas Merton" (I read his book *The Seven Storey Mountain*), and other chapters that gave me wonderful insights into the life of a hermit—but *In the Spirit of Happiness* was an inside look at the spiritual life of a contemporary Catholic monastic order that spoke to the spiritual needs of our time; and as I waited for my friend to do her business I read the Preface, Authors' Note, and Chapter One: "The Seeker," and I was hooked; so I bought it.

I've only got two more chapters to go, and I'm very grateful for the opportunity to get a look into the spiritually disciplined life of a modern monastic Catholic order because it gave me an insight into Catholicism that I needed to round off my understanding of my old Roman Catholic faith, which for reasons much too deep to explain here was terribly skewed by my New Age spirituality—but which my spiritual healing sessions with you set straight, and for which I am ever so grateful!

If I may Padre, let me wax philosophical a moment about my relationship with my old Roman Catholic faith and my relationship with you, which came as a COMPLETE SURPRISE to me. But strangely enough, you did tell me in my last spiritual healing session that you and I had planned on the Other Side before we came into the world to work together to help raise the spiritual consciousness of the world, but I had a long journey to make before I was ready to meet you through my spiritual sensitive last year! My God, what a journey it was just to get to the point where we could work together on my book *Healing with Padre Pio*!

The point I want to make is that my relationship with my Catholic faith grew out of a misunderstanding of the spirituality of this great religion founded upon the teachings of Jesus, and I had to go through hell to find my way out of the labyrinthine nonsense of the false premises of my faith (like eternal damnation in hell, to name the most psychically damaging)—and I came out bitter and angry at Christianity. So bitter and angry that I needed the healing grace of a Roman Catholic Saint who had suffered the holy wounds of Jesus for fifty years to heal my wounded Christian soul!

Again, thank you Padre. As I said in *Healing with Padre Pio*, we began with the premise of healing my wounded Christian soul, but we ended up healing the wounded soul of Christianity, and finally the wounded soul of the world with the healing grace of your consciousness of all knowing and all seeing. I simply proved to be the medium for your healing grace, and I feel privileged to continue being of service to your mission of serving life from the Other Side.

Padre, you did say in one of the books that I read on your life that you would do more for humanity from the Other Side (actually, you used the word heaven) than you could do while you were in your suffering body, and given the testimonials that I read of all the miracles that people from all over the world have attributed to you, it seems that you were right—not to mention what you are doing with me! But just what are you doing with me? Let's look at this for a moment…

I believe you are allowing me to offer the world the very UNIQUE PERSPECTIVE of a Roman Catholic Saint who has transcended the inflexible doctrine of Roman Catholicism and realized spiritual ascendancy into the Soul Plane of Consciousness of all knowing and all seeing, thereby allowing the world to see that all spiritual paths come from what you have symbolically revealed to me as the River of God that flows into different streams and which we impede by placing our "rocks" of misunderstanding into our individual stream; and it's your duty in your service to God to help us become aware of our spiritual impasses so we can continue on our journey home to God. But of course you know very well how Roman Catholics are going to respond to this.

This is going to be very controversial; but as you said in one of my sessions when I brought this up, "controversy is good because it causes dialogue"—and the world is in desperate need of a new dialogue on Christianity, which Bishop John Shelby Spong is trying to initiate with books like *Why Christianity Must Change or Die*, and *Jesus for the Non-Religious*. I know my book *Healing with Padre Pio* is a novel, but I had to couch my spiritual healing sessions with you into a story of fiction, because that's the only way I could have the freedom to explore our process together.

Controversial or not then, I'm writing you these letters for personal reasons and what happens thereafter will be up to Providence. I've since come to see that my life is choreographed from above, and all I can do is play my little part and hope for the best; so whether people like this privileged glimpse into your life as an Ascended Spiritual Master or not, it's not really for me to say. All I can do is work out the thoughts and ideas that I am given to express creatively through my writing, and I know that this epistolary project is going to prove very, very satisfying.

Before I close, I'm going to make a personal request. I know that we have to be specific in our requests from Divine Spirit, and I'm going to be specific in my invocation (being an Ascended Master, I know that you are one with Divine Spirit): please let my published books begin to bear fruit soon, because it's causing Penny and me a great deal of anxiety waiting for all the good karma that we have put into getting my books written and published to reap some financial benefits—my latest book being *Keeper of the Flame,* which came out last month.

Last night we picked up a coffee at Tim Hortons and went for a long drive to talk things out (we do this often just to air our head), and we discussed the possibility of having to move back up north into our triplex (we have two units rented, which go towards the mortgage on the house; we used to live on the top unit) and sell our house down here in Georgian Bay to finance our retirement; but as realistic as I am and would concede to the idea, I don't want to, and neither does Penny. So Padre, if you would, please intercede, because I honestly don't know what else we can do to make it happen.

I pour my heart and soul into my writing, and Penny pours her heart and soul into editing, formatting, and getting my books out, doing book trailers and promoting and marketing them wherever she can on the Internet—after her work day and on weekends!

Penny's invaluable to my writing, and I don't know what I would do without her; but we are getting on in years, and we are getting concerned. I only wish I did not have to have bypass surgery three years ago. It put a serious damper on our finances, and we're hoping that one of my books connects before our savings run out; so, again, please see what you can do to remove those obstacles that are keeping my books from connecting with the readers that I know are out there waiting to read them.

I trust you Padre. Given what I experienced with my spiritual healing sessions, I believe in you; but Penny hasn't quite rapped her mind around my relationship with you yet, and I have to be patient. She is my heart and soul, and my love for her only grows deeper with each new day, and the last thing I want is to burden her with the anxiety of financial struggle in our old age. Let it happen Padre, before it's too late.

I remain,
Your faithful companion,
Orest

4. THE WHOLE WORLD'S ASLEEP

Letters to Ascended Master
St. Padre Pio,
Wednesday, July 27, 2011
6: 45 A. M.

Dear Padre,

I finished reading *In the Spirit of Happiness* by the Monks of New Skete yesterday, my favorite chapter being "What Does Love Look Like," which I'm going to pursue in another letter or spiritual musing, or both; but this morning I want to share my thoughts on something that the Seeker (who is a composite character made up of pilgrims that went to New Skete) said to Father Laurence, the founder of the Orthodox Catholic monastic order of New Skete in Cambridge, New York.

The Seeker had corresponded with Father Laurence and wanted to meet him in person, so he flew to New York to visit New Skete, and Father Laurence picked him up at the airport. On the drive to the monastery, Father said, "How about telling me a bit about yourself," which the Seeker did; and when he stopped talking, Father said, "And what have you learned through all of this?"

The Seeker thought before replying. Finally, he said, "I've learned that the whole world's asleep—including myself."

If I may, I'd like to explore this concept of being asleep to life, which is the dominant theme of all spiritual paths...

Jesus came into the world to wake us up from the deep sleep of life, but you really took me by surprise in one of my spiritual healing sessions when you told me that Jesus came from the future. That blew my mind!

It took a while for this to sink in, and then I asked if you would tell me where the world was headed if Jesus had to come back from the future to wake the world up from its deep sleep. Was the world headed too far off its spiritual course for its own good and the Spiritual Hierarchy had to intervene by sending Jesus to troubleshoot the world with his salvation teaching? I asked; but you wouldn't tell me.

You said that had to do with the finer inner workings of the universe, and it was not for me to know at this time; but now I'd like to explore this concept with you of being asleep to life, because I believe the world has veered off spiritual course again and there is a great spiritual intervention happening even as I write this letter—which was confirmed by the book that Providence brought to my front door by my neighbor, *The Only Planet of Choice,* by Phyllis V. Schlemmer: the Nine Silent Ones said that the world is in danger of destroying itself. And if I may be allowed to say this, I believe you are one of the Ascended Masters that is intervening to help steer the world back on its spiritual course—hence, your coming to my Medical Intuitive three years ago so we could meet and work on *Healing with Padre Pio,* which will help to wake the world up from its profound spiritual stupor.

But what do I mean by "profound spiritual stupor," because that's how I see the world? The Seeker told Father Laurence that his searching had led him to believe that the whole world was asleep, including himself; but I see this sleep as a profound spiritual stupor. Not that there isn't something profoundly spiritual going on in the world, which I believe there is because I'm a part of this spiritual awakening, but as I told you in one of my sessions, I believe the soul of the world has become much too big for the ego of the world, and something has to give—like grass growing through asphalt!

This is why the world is going through a spiritual cleansing with all of these earthquakes and tsunamis and violent hurricanes and floods and forest fires and droughts and crop failures and famine and world climate changes that are forcing humanity to wake up to our relationship with our environment. We simply can't continue the way we are, because we're headed for disaster. This is what you told me these world disasters were all about—waking us up to our spiritual responsibilities!

But why this profound spiritual stupor? What's the root cause of this deep life-sleep? Why do we refuse to wake up?

Padre, I've given this a lot of thought in my novels, and especially in my spiritual musings, and I've come to the conclusion that we have reached the limits of our ego potential; we simply cannot gorge ourselves any longer on the pleasures of life and expect not to pay a price for our indulgence. This is what the Nine Enlightened Ones in *The Only Planet of Choice* said. Earth is the only planet of desire, and man has become so greedy with desire that he has forgotten his spiritual purpose in life, so they have to intervene.

This is why the world is experiencing all these natural catastrophes. It's the only way to wake the world up from its profound spiritual stupor. In a word, the ego of the world has gone mad and something has to give; but ego is terrified of waking up to our responsibility to the world, and it's doing all it can to keep us asleep to life!

Fear is the root cause of this profound spiritual stupor; the fear of having to sacrifice some of that boundless desire and assume our responsibility to the world we have created, and I can see this profound spiritual stupor whenever I go on Facebook. I cannot believe our preoccupation with the "good life" and the thousand and one struggles that this life of self-indulgence is heir to; and we refuse to acknowledge anything that threatens our spiritual stupor—like my spiritual musings on "old whore life."

But you did tell me to speak only to those who have ears for what I have to say, and which I finally understand now; so what am I to do?

I'm certainly not going to stop writing my spiritual musings, because they are a phenomenal way to tap into the higher consciousness of life; but if I don't start attracting readers who resonate with my writing—or, if you will, people like the Seeker who wants to wake up to life, I'm going to get pretty discouraged. Can you do anything about that? Can you start bringing those people to my books?

You did say that I shouldn't worry about this, because it was your job and God's job to bring readers to my books; but "at my back I hear time's winged chariot drawing near," and I'd like to see some fruit for all my labor before it's too late; if not for me, for Penny's sake. Penny's belief in me keeps me going, but some days can be very trying.

Enough whining. Thank you for listening, Padre. I just wanted to let you know that I'm grateful to you for bringing *In the Spirit of Happiness* into my life. It gave me a wonderful insight into spiritual growth through a community of like-minded people, and a glimpse into the monastic order of your Capuchin community.

Oh, I should mention (not that you don't already know) that the New Skete monastic order is an offshoot of the Franciscan Order. The Capuchin Order, which you belonged to, is a Franciscan Order; and this is just another one of those little coincidences that have become so common in my life from the day I began my spiritual healing sessions with you!

In fact, so common and in greater proximity to each other are these coincidences happening in my life that I have the terrifying thought that I am approaching what Jesus called the "Holy Now" in Glenda Green's book *Love Without End, Jesus Speaks*: "In the state of hypersynchronicity" (the Holy Now), cause and effect are the same. As awareness departs from the sacred point, cause and effect are observed to be complimentary..." (p. 288). Wow! Is this where I'm headed?

I remain,
Your faithful companion,
Orest

5. EXPERIENCING THE HOLY NOW WITH MY NEIGHBORS

Letters to Ascended Master
St. Padre Pio,
Thursday, July 28, 2011
9: 25 A. M.

Dear Padre,

I don't know if I'm reading too much into this (perhaps because I wish it to be true), but I think yesterday you gave me a deeper glimpse into the hypersynchronistic potential of my life (i.e., approaching the Holy Now) with an experience with my next door neighbor who brought her children up to the family cottage.

Her three children are boys, the youngest two years old, the other six, and the oldest ten. I went bike riding with the two older boys one evening, and the next day the middle boy came over to the house to ask if we could go bike riding again, and we did; and later as I was reading on my front deck the three boys came over to join me.

Their mother speaks Italian fluently, and I asked her the day before if she could write in Italian, which she can; so I wanted to know if she could translate a couple of short paragraphs into Italian for my novel *Healing with Padre Pio*. These were the two questions that I asked you in my poor Italian dialect in one of my spiritual healing sessions.She said she would, and I told her I'd bring them over the next day, or the day after. I didn't want to impose on her right away. I wanted her to enjoy her first few days at the cottage with her children.

After dinner last night I was on the front deck reading *Lost Books Of The Bible,* by William Hone (the books that were left out of the Bible; I was reading St. Paul's Letters that were not included in the Bible) when I heard the boys outside. They had just finished dinner and had come out to play.

Their two cousins, both girls, had come to the cottage with their mother, just for the day; and they were all excited to be together and wanted to get as much play time in before the mother and girls left that evening. They had to return early because they were moving into their new house and a lot had to be done. The girls were not happy to be moving to a new neighborhood in Toronto because they would miss their friends.

In any event, as I was sitting there the thought occurred to me to drop over with the two paragraphs that I wanted translated because I thought the two sisters could work on it together and give me the best translation possible; so I got my paper and walked over.

Of course, I had to explain what I wanted translated, which entailed telling them about my spiritual healing sessions with you; but they weren't as shocked as I thought they would be. They're Roman Catholic, with a very deep faith in their religion that got badly shaken when their father died of cancer five years ago.

The whole family was angry at God because they did not think it was fair for their father to be taken so early, and their anger had not gone away, which gave me the opportunity to introduce the concepts of karma and reincarnation that I expound upon in *Healing with Padre*

Pio; and after I told them about how my Medical Intuitive, who is a spiritual sensitive (a modern term for psychic medium) channeled you for my sessions one of the girls told me about their parish priest who was also spiritually gifted and who left his parish to go to a smaller parish where he was "called" to pursue his gift by doing "healing Masses" for parishioners.

This priest married my neighbor and her husband, who had a near-fatal car accident and who swears that St. Anthony saved his life. In fact, when their priest was counseling them for marriage he saw that St. Anthony was in the room with the young man, and he commented on the Saint's presence; so the young man told him about his accident and how his mother prayed to St. Anthony to spare his life. This story made it easier for me to share my experience with you, Padre, and it also gave me the opportunity to give the girls a copy of my new novel *Keeper of the Flame,* which is sure to expand their spiritual horizons.

Now I can make my point, which I hope is not too tenuous (for me, it's not; but for the reader it might appear that I'm trying to pour the ocean into a teacup), and it is this: while standing at the kitchen sink doing the dishes, the mother of the three boys was telling her sister what wonderful neighbors Penny and I were, how lucky they were to have us for neighbors, and she was wondering what she could do for us—and just then I appeared at the door with my two paragraphs for her to translate into Italian!

Coincidence? I think not. I think this experience was proof of what I am beginning to see as the Holy Now—that mystifying concept of "singularity" that Jesus tries to explain to Glenda Green in her book *Love Without End, Jesus Speaks:*

"Due to the one spirit and the highly integrated, synchronistic nature of all existence, there is an aspect of singularity, although it is not a particle or point. It is a function of hypersynchronicity which can compress any or every part of existence to a singular state of infinite potential. Thus, 'singularity' as an aspect of separation does not exist. Separation is not honored to that degree" (p. 289).

This is such a deep concept that it is beyond my comprehension, and yet I think I do perceive it; and my experience with my neighbor was your way of giving me proof that I am approaching the Holy Now, which is accessed by hypersynchronstic experiences like my experience with my neighbor when she thought of something she could do for her wonderful neighbors and I showed up at her door at precisely that moment with the paragraphs that I wanted her to translate for me!

Was existence, hers and mine, compressed to a point of singularity? Did we experience the Holy Now where cause and effect were one? Was this a moment of "perfect stasis," as Jesus explained it: *"The universe is implicitly and explicitly of one piece. At the point of perfect stasis between the implicit and explicit, there is a condition of hypersynchronicity where matter, energy, space, and time move into a 'no-resistance' mode of infinite potential. This is not the collapse of matter. This is the synchronizing of it to a 'zero point' of perfect stasis* (Stasis, He explained, is the perfect repose of hypersynchronicity.) *Understand that 'zero point' is not about 'nothingness.' It's a designation of infinity"* (p. 287).

Isn't this "designation of infinity" the Holy Now, the Eternal Present, that place where cause and effect are one?

This is deep stuff, Padre; but I think that these letters have opened me up to a greater flow of Divine Spirit, and my doors of perception have been opened enough for me to catch a glimpse of the Holy Now in the experiences of my daily life! Wow!

Now that I have shared this with you (it seems foolish that I should speak like this, because you are ever-present in my life and know everything about me; but I will talk about this in another letter), let me share a dream I had a month or so ago of being so present in the Holy Now that I became a magnet for people. I had such spiritual gravitas in my dream that people couldn't get enough of me! In my dream, I *knew* that I was living in the moment—the Holy Now!

Is the inner starting to manifest on the outer? I think so, but I don't want to go there yet because that's too much for me to think about. It terrifies me to know that I'm getting that close to the "singularity"!

I remain,
Your faithful companion,
Orest

6. WALKING A TIGHTROPE WITH PADRE PIO

Letters to Ascended Master
St. Padre Pio,
Sunday, July 31, 2011
9: 50 A. M.

Dear Padre,

I just finished writing another spiritual musing ("A New Species of Man: Homo Luminous") for my second volume of musings (*Old Whore Life: Exploring the Shadow Side of Karma*) and which I will be posting on my blog eventually, but I still feel spiritually restless; hence my letter to you this morning.

Before the spirit of this letter carries me away, let me thank you for coming to my aid the other night. I was beseeched by that sexual consciousness that I am prone to every once in a while (I was living in France in my early twenties and I accidentally opened up the chakra at the base of my spine while meditating one evening and awakened the *kundalini* energy, and I've had issues with my sexual energy ever since; thank goodness I learned to sublimate it through Gurdjieff's teaching of "work on oneself" and creative writing), and I repeated one of my spiritual power mantras to safeguard me from the temptations of my libidinous consciousness (in your earthly lifetime you called these temptations the "devil" but now call them one's "personal demons"), and I felt immediate relief from the downward pull of these unconscious desires; so, thank you.

In all honesty, I had no idea that you would become such a big part of my life when I started my project *Healing with Padre Pio*. I did not expect for you to be always present in my life. But being one with Divine Spirit it was only logical that you would be with me all the time because I asked for your help for my spiritual healing; and I'm grateful now that you are always with me because you affect spiritual change in me that would otherwise take a long time to realize without your energy, for such is my resonance with you!

I did laugh however when you told me that I didn't have to be so much on my guard that I would be too afraid to live my life. You said my consciousness of your presence in my life was like walking a tightrope and that I should not be afraid to fall off every now and then; and you know what, that's exactly how I feel I'm living my life now—on a tightrope!

And I was afraid of falling off the other night. That's why I called for your help. And instantly I felt your energy drive away my sexual demons. What a relief that was!

Now, perhaps I should explore this whole concept of being assailed by one's demons. First, what are one's demons anyway?

My perception is that one's demons are archetypal energies that have merged to form a matrix of unconscious ego-energy (what Carl Jung called our shadow) that seeks to feed off our conscious ego energies by forcing us to give them expression; hence, the more we give in to our demons, the more power our unconscious shadow self has over us.

In other words, our demons are of our own making; although, we do inherit many of these archetypal patterns from our parents. This is what is meant by the sins of the parents being visited upon the children and grandchildren.

It is not the sins of our parents as such that are passed on to us, but the archetypal patterns of their sins; or, to express it differently, their shadow becomes a part of our personal shadow, or unconscious self.

So as we resolve our shadow self, we help our parents in their growth to spiritual enlightenment. What a mystery life is, isn't it Padre? But we just keep plugging along. I think that's all I want to say for today.

I remain,
Your faithful companion,
Orest

7. WHAT DOES LOVE LOOK LIKE?

Letters to Ascended Master
St. Padre Pio,
Monday, August 1, 2011
7:40 A. M.

Dear Padre,

I've just been re-reading the chapter "What Does Love Look Like" in the book *In the Spirit of Happiness* by the Monks of New Skete, because I wanted to refresh my memory so I could write a spiritual musing on this fascinating question, but for some reason I feel like sharing my thoughts on love with you; hence my letter this morning.

I can't get the memory of my neighbor's three young boys, especially the two youngest, out of my mind. The boys came up with their mother to their family cottage next door to our house (the cottage is shared by her two siblings and young families), but the boys spent much of their time on my front deck with me.

I love reading on the front deck of our house, so I've been spending a lot of time there in the summers since my bypass operation three years ago. Before my bypass I had to work my trade of drywall taping and painting because summer was my busiest time of year, but I'm only picking up small jobs now and I spend many summer afternoons on my deck reading books that I'm called upon to read—like *In the Spirit of Happiness,* which I felt compelled to read for my book of letters to you; so the boys would see me on the deck and come over to visit and talk, and share, and play.

I mention this because it was like the boys, especially the two young ones, just couldn't get enough of my energy. They wanted to touch me and sit on me and be close to me. I said to Penny, "I've got my spiritual gravitas back!"

That's how I used to attract children when I was loaded with spiritual energy when I was consumed by my quest for my true self and employed every technique I could to gather and collect spiritual energy, because I had learned that to be my true self I had to grow in my true self, and to grow in my true self I had to harness all the spiritual energy that I could get; and I harnessed so much energy that I attracted children like bees to honey. One seven year old boy even came down to my house one evening after dinner and knocked on our door and asked my mother if I could come out to play!

This was the most endearing gesture of innocence that I have ever experienced, and this is what the young boys next door reminded me of every time they walked over to be with me on the front deck; but so intrigued was I by their attraction to my energy that I asked Penny, "Why does my energy attract children and repel most adults?"

"It's their innocence," she replied, without thought. "They don't have anything to hide from you. Most adults have something to hide, and they can't stand to be around you because your energy threatens their falseness."

I had to agree with her. In fact, something you said at one of my spiritual healing sessions confirmed this. Remember, Padre? I asked you why I affected one member of my spiritual community the way I did. "She has a hate on for me like you wouldn't believe," I said, and you replied that it was because I saw something in her that she did not want to face up to, and I threatened what she pretended to be—i.e., a kind and loving person. Which brings me right back to the theme of this letter—what does love look like?

"Love looks like generosity," said Father Laurence. **"It spends itself willingly (and wisely) for others, be it with time, attention, money, or simply concern"** (*In the Spirit of Happiness,* p. 255). That's the face of love that I would like to explore in my letter this morning, and the woman that I threatened is a perfect example of the kind of person who makes out like she's all about love but her behavior speaks otherwise.

Didn't Jesus say, *"Wherefore by their fruits ye shall know them?"* (Math. 7: 20). Well, I listened to what this woman had to say and then observed her behavior. She loved to humiliate her husband in public at our spiritual functions until I finally called her up on it one day because I could no longer suffer her husband's humiliation, telling her to keep her marital dynamic private and not bring it to our functions; and another time I told her how gauche it was to bring her own food into a restaurant, which she often did after one of our spiritual functions. I saw her shadow, and she hated me for it.

Of course, you told me to be more accepting and kinder in my response to her, and not embarrass her by challenging her, and I took your advice. Not that I wanted to, but because I knew that this was all part of my own spiritual healing—which culminated in the slaying of my overweening spiritual conceit by the devastating power of your humility!

In any event, the point I want to make is that the face of love that I wanted to explore this morning speaks to the generosity of love, which is a face that I'm very familiar with because I learned a long time ago that giving of oneself—be it in time, concern, or coin—is one of the most satisfying ways to grow spiritually, and one of the most obvious.

I can always tell if a person has love in their heart by how they give of themselves, and I've come to the conclusion that the cheaper one is (in their time, concern, or coin) the less love they have in their heart. For me, this is a mathematical certainty!

That's all for today, Padre. I hope I didn't invite a new spiritual lesson here, as I often do when I speak my mind so frankly.

I remain,
Your faithful companion,
Orest

8. ACTIONS SPEAK LOUDER THAN WORDS

Letters to Ascended Master
St. Padre Pio,
Sunday, August 7, 2011
5:35 A. M.

Dear Padre,

Yesterday Penny and I attended our monthly Spiritual Discourse class in a small community north of Barrie. We usually attend these classes in Orillia, but a member of our group wanted to hold a potluck lunch after our class at her home by the river, so we decided to hold the class there yesterday, and it was a beautiful day.

We didn't know what we were going to bring for potluck lunch. Penny thought of making a Wisconsin Strawberry Pie (she had just made one for my birthday), but she opted for a big bowl of potato salad instead, enough for a dozen people; and I decided to make Italian Bruschetta for an appetizer because I had picked up a basket of fresh field tomatoes at Johnson's Market in Midland, and I sliced up enough French baguette so everyone could have at least two pieces of Bruschetta.

Penny made her potato salad the night before, and I made the Bruschetta early Saturday morning because I had to toast the slices of baguette.

We held our class outdoors in the back yard overlooking the river with the occasional pontoon boat and canoe floating up or down the river, and it was one of the best classes we've ever had. There were the seven regular members in our class, plus one guest from southern Ontario who was a friend of the lady hosting the potluck (she had been invited to stay the weekend), and there was plenty of discussion on the Spiritual Discourse.

After the class we served ourselves the potluck buffet. There was no main entrée, because no one had brought one (the hostess's contribution to the potluck was a small chocolate cake), one lady brought a small pasta salad, another lady with a giving heart brought a specially prepared rice dish and plate of veggies and dip (she's on a strict diet for health reasons and just wanted to make sure she would have something she could eat), Penny had her potato salad, I added my Bruschetta, and the hostess's husband went out and bought some fresh corn while we were doing our class and his wife steamed half a dozen cut in half immediately after class, another lady brought a small bowl of fruit salad made of chunks of watermelon and a few blueberries and fewer strawberries, and the last member of the class, who is a newcomer to the teaching, didn't bring anything; and there was water, tea, and coffee for beverages. That was it.

Padre, I don't know how to broach this subject without pushing some buttons (which I think deserve to be pushed), but I have to because it speaks to the nature of love—or, more precisely, to the paucity of love.

If you remember in my last letter ("What Does Love Look Like?") I quoted the Monks of New Skete who said, **"love looks like generosity,"** but generosity is not a virtue that Penny and I have witnessed very often since we moved to Georgian Bay. In fact it is so well hidden that I don't think people would recognize it if they saw it; or, rather, to be perfectly honest, they would be shocked by it—as Penny and I witnessed when we held a potluck harvest turkey dinner at our house for the members of our spiritual community the first year we moved here. They couldn't believe the bounty of our table.

This quality about people that we've witnessed more often than we would care to admit (I don't know what to call it; perhaps thrift, cheapness, or parsimony of spirit) never ceases to astonish us. What would it have taken to barbeque a few hot dogs as a main entrée for our potluck lunch after class? The cost would've been minimal, and it was a great day for a barbeque by the river. Or lasagna as a main entrée would have gone a long way to satisfying the guests. I've picked up lasagnas on sale for Penny and myself for well under ten dollars, and one would have been enough to feed our whole class. That wouldn't have been asking too much, would it?

As Penny said, the host has an obligation; but that doesn't seem to apply for some people. Another time we attended a potluck lunch at another member of our spiritual community's house, on the same river before she relocated after her husband died, and she had a package of twelve tiny pastry appetizers for her contribution. Thank goodness some members brought enough for everybody. Penny brought a pot full of homemade cabbage rolls, but the hostess didn't want to turn on the oven to heat them up because it was going to use up too much electricity and Penny had to heat them in a frying pan—*and our spiritual path is supposed to be about love!*

"Love spends itself willingly for others, be it with time, attention, money, or simply concern," said the Monks of New Skete—which reminds me of the little incident of how you showed your love one day when you mentioned to your doctor friend (Dr. Mario De Giacomo) that you were fond of *spaghetti ala napoletana* the way your mother made it and it had been years since you had it last, and out of his great love for you your doctor friend had a lady prepare you a nice big plate and he brought it to you the next day; but as much as you wanted to eat it, you asked your doctor friend to give it to one of the poor peasants who would enjoy the meal much more than you.

Padre, your little sacrifice of the simple plate of one of your favorite dishes speaks to the generosity of your soul, and for my money it was an act of pure grace. *That's what love is supposed to look like!*

I don't want to say any more about the paucity of love that Penny and I have witnessed down here, especially in our own spiritual community (an irony difficult to support because it begs judgment), except for one little point that Penny made. "Love comes from the heart, not the mouth," she said.

Indeed, actions speak louder than words!

I remain,
Your faithful companion,
Orest

9. THE MANY DIMENSIONS OF SPIRITUALITY

Letters to Ascended Master
St. Padre Pio,
Wednesday, Aug.10, 2011
6:10 A.M.

Dear Padre,

While Penny and I were doing our spiritual contemplation last night, the thought came to me to post my letters to you on a blog. I already have a blog for my spiritual musings, but the thought came through to post my letters to you.

I ran it by Penny, and after our contemplation she read my first two letters to you and smiled, then chuckled because she found them rather revealing; especially when I talk about my propensity to procrastinate. "You should read this letter every week to remind yourself," she said, and laughed. Thank goodness for her patience.

I've decided to think about it. I don't want to jump right in because it would mean a commitment. I have the pressure of writing a spiritual musing every week on top of working on my current novel and getting my first book of musings ready to be published, so before I commit myself to posting my letters to you on a new blog site I'd like to have at least twenty or so letters already written so I don't put myself behind the eight ball.

Last night when I went to sleep I asked if I could meet you in my dreams. "Give me something interesting for my letters," I said, hoping to entice you into my dreams; but I should know better. **Spirit does what Spirit wills**, and all I can hope for is a happy coincidence of my will coinciding with Spirit's will. In any event, Penny and I talked over the possibilities of posting my letters because we think it would be a great way to get more exposure; but more importantly, it would offer Christian readers an outside-the-box perspective on the many dimensions of spirituality.

But do they want to know about the many dimensions of spirituality? I get the feeling they don't. I can't help but feel that people today are in a strange place. They are being forced to wake up because of world events, but the responsibility that comes with greater consciousness forces them to try to stay asleep a little longer, spiritually speaking.

There's a great resistance to acknowledge what's going on in the world. I was rereading *The Only Planet of Choice* yesterday, and the spokesman for the Nine Enlightened Beings said that we are all individually responsible for the state of the world, but this is too much for people to bear, and so they prefer not to wake up; hence, the obsessive preoccupation with the little self.

"It is because people are frightened to find out who they really are," said Tom, the spokesman for the Nine Enlightened Beings, "for when they know that completely, they feel the responsibility is too great" (p. 269).

This fear of self-knowledge keeps people spiritually asleep.

But to keep the world from self-destruction we have to wake up and "remove self from self," said Tom, which we also discussed in my chapter "The Selfless Self" in *Healing with Padre Pio*; but this is not a concept that will soon catch fire because the self is much too entrenched in its own needs, desires, and daily struggles. Indeed, life has to get very difficult before people wake up to their spiritual responsibility to themselves and the world at large. I'm sure we can expect more catastrophes and political upheavals.

So should I post my letters? I have one concern that bothers me (aside from how readers might respond), and that has to do with maintaining the integrity of my letters, because you can rest assured that I will have one eye on my reader as I open myself up to you. It's my intention to open up my heart to you with these letters, because I want to grow in spirit, and there's no better way to grow in spirit than to open up one's heart; fear however may keep me from being as frank as I want to be.

Indeed, fear is the bugaboo of spiritual growth, isn't it? We have to talk about this in my next book with you. I don't know when this is going to be. I thought we would be starting it next spring, but it looks more like next fall or winter now because I have to get *Healing with Padre Pio* out before we begin our next project with the woman who channeled you, and I don't think we can get it out before spring. But it's all choreographed from above, isn't it Padre? So why worry?

Just do what we have to do and let the day unfold as it will. That seems to be the way to live in the moment. I only wish it were as simple as that. Maybe it is. Maybe I'm just not getting it. I'd sure love to meet someone who lives in the moment. Maybe I've already met them and didn't recognize that they live in the moment. What would characterize them?

I'm doing a lot of blathering this morning, aren't I? I have to leave at 7:30 for an eight o'clock appointment at Canadian Tire for my van. I blew my muffler the other day. I may need a whole new tailpipe, I don't know; but this is the third thing that's happened to me that is going to cost us.

I may have cracked a tooth two weeks ago, because I still can't bite on it; so I have a dentist appointment this Friday and may be looking at a root canal. We don't have a dental plan, so there's an unexpected expense, and our lawn tractor broke down and is getting repaired. We had work done on it last year to the tune of six hundred dollars, and it's not even four years old. I know, that's life; but does it have to gang up on us?

Same day, 7 P.M....

Padre, I got a break on my muffler. I didn't blow my muffler, or my tailpipe; they had to replace a flange that had rusted out. Labor and material came to $111.00, which is far better than what I expected; and I had an interesting experience while waiting for my van.

A customer waiting for his vehicle, whose name was Don, talked about his life. It started with my comment about getting a break on my muffler, which opened the door for how many times he had been "screwed royally" in his life (great material for my book *Old Whore Life*), and I listened to his incredible story of misadventure for half an hour or more, and what a story it was! But throughout his story he kept telling me that he could not compromise himself— which cost him his military career!

I told him he should write a novel.

"Yeah, everybody tells me that," he said, but I think the whole point of me being there with him was to let him experience your presence with me, and I know you will be working on him now; so, Padre, I did my part and introduced him to your energy, and I wish him the best on his journey through life.

Then I drove into Barrie to visit my friend at her bookstore, and guess what? I ended up exchanging my novel *Keeper of the Flame* with a clinical psychologist from Wasaga Beach who was dropping off some copies of her own book to sell on consignment. Her book is called *The Gifts of Responsibility,* and from her bio I learned that she was a Roman Catholic who expanded the horizons of her faith. Her book interests me very much, and I will share my feelings with you when I've read it. Incidentally, Padre, I think you brought this book into my life for my spiritual growth.

I also had a long conversation in the bookstore with two other ladies, one in her fifties and the other in her eighties, and for some reason both needed to make the point that they had to be true to themselves—which brought to mind what I said this morning about meeting people who live in the moment. Did I get my answer? Do we live in the moment by being true to ourselves? Is this the message you tried to give me today with all these people who talked about how they had to be true to themselves?

I'll have to do a spiritual musing on this…

I remain,
Your faithful companion,
Orest

10. THE RIVER OF GOD

Letters to Ascended Master
St. Padre Pio,
Thursday, August 11, 2011
8: 45 A. M.

Dear Padre,

Okay, Penny and I thought it over and this morning decided I should go ahead with a new blog; but Penny wasn't comfortable with the title I had chosen for my book of letters to you, so we tried a variety of titles until we came upon a working title that we both agreed upon: *The River Of God, Private Letters to Ascended Master St. Padre Pio.* "There," she said; "now you can have your cake and eat it, too." She said that because I wanted to keep "Ascended Master" in my title, which she didn't like (she still can't wrap her mind around my relationship with you), and she wanted the word "personal" in the title, but we settled on "private" because it's catchier. What do you think?

Penny thought the image of a river would catch the reader's attention, and I agreed because it makes reference to the River of God that you spoke of in my sessions with you, the image of the Divine Current that flows from God to create life and carry souls back home to God. You went into more detail though. You used the image of one placing a big stone in the River of God, which impeded the flow of the Divine Current in his life, like the huge boulder that I had created with my spiritual conceit that impeded the flow of the Divine Current in my life—hence my healing brought about by your sanctifying grace!

I've thanked you already for my spiritual healing, Padre; but I'd like to thank you again because my sessions with you changed my life. Like I said to my friend at her bookstore yesterday, "I feel such an enormous relief since my healing sessions with Padre Pio. You don't realize how heavy ego can be until you're relieved of its weight upon your soul. Honest to God, I think ego has to be the most burdensome thing in the world!"

I wanted to throw up at the thought of my pre-Padre Pio life; that's how disgusted I was with my spiritual conceit. Had I not been slain by your humility I would still be out there blindly strutting my stuff like the spiritual peacock that I was! This reminds me of the comment made by the Spiritual Traveler Rebazar Tarzs about Jesus strutting his stuff like a peacock—not to compare myself with Jesus, though. God forbid!

No; all I want to do is show that we are all blind to our own vanity—our own "stone" in the River of God that impedes the flow of the Divine Current of Love in our life, and I'm sure that Jesus had his moments.

That's what the River of God is, an endless current of Love that flows from God and back to God. Jesus called it the "water of everlasting life," and as it flows from God it creates and sustains life, and as it flows back to God it awakens and returns soul back home a spiritually self-realized, God conscious soul ready to serve in the Divine Plan of God as you are doing by helping souls on their journey through life.

Padre, how did you know that you would do more to help mankind from Heaven than you were doing in your humble role as a Capuchin monk who said Mass every morning and listened to over one hundred confessions every day, not to mention your personal response to the many letters that people wrote you, when you were allowed to respond that is?

Your superiors, whom you obeyed absolutely because of your vow of obedience, denied you this precious gift of service for a period of time; but I don't want to get into that here. Suffice to say that I know how much you had to suffer to simply serve your fellow man, but serve you did; and now you are serving from the Other Side in your capacity as an Ascended Master and I can't thank you enough for bringing me together with the woman who channeled you so that we could do a book on spiritual healing. And when I asked if we would meet again you said that our work was not done yet.

Did you anticipate this book of letters? I did ask if we would be doing another book with my spiritual sensitive, and you said yes, and I even caught a glimpse of the theme of this new project which was inspired by *Ecclesiastes*; but it never occurred to me to write you a series of letters until a few weeks ago when I was reading on our front deck.

The thought came to me out of the blue, but I know you planted that seed in my mind, and it didn't take long to take root because I've always wanted to write a book of letters; and just the other night as Penny and I were doing our spiritual contemplation you planted the seed in my mind to create a new blog for my letters and share them with the public before I publish them in book form!

Once again, I had no thought of posting them on a blog site. That idea came to me out of the blue also, and I know you gave it to me; so Penny and I have decided to go ahead with it, and when she comes back from her trip up north where she's going for her niece's wedding (and to visit her father), she will create my new blog site for me because I don't have a clue how to go about it and I can begin posting my letters to you.

When you're called to serve, you're called aren't you? I almost feel like I felt when I caught my first scent of the Way and had to follow it like the hound of Heaven in Thompson's poem. I had to go wherever the scent took me, and believe me it took me to places that taught me lessons I will never forget—like that offshoot Christian solar cult teaching allegedly brought into the world by a "Child Christ" that did irreparable damage to my eyesight! But I can't bring myself to talk about that now.

Strangely enough however, the thought came to me just yesterday to dig out my old manuscript of the novel I had started to write on my experience with that diabolical offshoot Christian solar cult teaching that I studied for three years.

I never think about this novel, because the thought of reliving that experience horrifies me. I called it *The Sunworshipper*, but the thought came to me yesterday to write it as the main story in a book of short stories, and it was almost strong enough for me to go to the basement and dig up my manuscript, but I didn't; so I guess you just planted the seed for now. But it would make a great story because it would reveal how far one will go to find his way back home to God—like risking one's eyesight as I did by burning three solar burns in the retina of my eyes with the techniques that this teaching taught so we could ingest the Logos supposedly imbued with the rays of the sun!

Wow! I still cringe at my experience. I couldn't write this novel because I couldn't relive the trauma of that whole experience, especially with my ophthalmologist who was so angry with me for doing those solar techniques that he dismissed me from his examining room and I had to fly down to the eye clinic in Waterloo for the appointment that my brother had arranged for me to find out how much damage I had done to my eyes.

But how could I explain to the ophthalmologist at the Thunder Bay Clinic the power of the Call of God? I could have asked him to read Thompson's poem "The Hound of Heaven," but what good would that have done? Nobody can understand a hound of heaven but another hound of heaven. "Rise, clasp my Hand, and come!" commands God, and I paid a dear price to be clasped by the Hand of God—as did you, Padre. God, I can't begin to fathom the pain you suffered for fifty years with the stigmata; but that was your choice. You did ask Jesus how you could serve his mission, and he gave you his five crucifixion wounds and you embraced *la via di sofferenza* so passionately that you said, "I want to inebriate myself with pain" because you couldn't suffer enough for Jesus. But why, the reader may ask? Why would one be so foolish to suffer like that? Where's the logic?

We could tell them, couldn't we? But I think I'll wait for another letter when I can delve into the mystery of what you called your "glory" and I came to call "virtue" and Jesus called storing our "treasures in heaven."

Indeed, the River of God has as many streams as there are souls in God's Kingdom. As you said, "life is a journey of the self." But mercifully, every stream will eventually find its way back into the River of God and flow back to the Godhead—*eureka!*

Didn't I say at the beginning of this project that this book of letters would find its own theme? Well, it just popped up—*the River of God!* This theme speaks to everyone, and it's going to be the working title for my book of letters to you!

I remain,
Your faithful companion,
Orest

11. A HOUND OF HEAVEN

Letters to Ascended Master
St. Padre Pio,
Friday, August 12, 2011
6: 50 A. M.

Dear Padre,

In my last letter I wrote something that I have to explore, because it will help to explain why spiritual seekers are driven the way they are and so hard to understand. I wrote: "Nobody can understand a hound of heaven but another hound of heaven."

We've all heard the expression "it takes one to know one." That's because they have a similar state of consciousness; or a similar frequency of vibrations, if you will. They resonate with their own kind, and a spiritual seeker has the consciousness of a spiritual seeker, which is why only a hound of heaven can understand a hound of heaven.

But that doesn't explain what a hound of heaven is, though; all it tells us is that spiritual seekers are different from the rest of the world. What makes them different; that's the question? What made me different? What made you different, Padre?

For that matter, what made the author of the new book (*The Gifts of Responsibility*) that you brought into my life yesterday different, because from what I've read so far I'd say that this author is also a hound of heaven?

Here's what happened. I was driving home from Midland yesterday when I got the urge to drive into Barrie to visit my friend at her bookstore. I picked up coffee at Tim Hortons on Bayfield for us, and as I sat behind the counter talking with my friend the author of *The Gifts of Responsibility* came into the store to drop off four copies of her newly published book for my friend to sell in her store. She also had a bag of used books that she wanted to sell to my friend, and as she put them onto the counter the title of one book jumped out—*The Disappearance of the Universe*, by Gary R. Reynard, the book I couldn't finish reading because I felt that something wasn't right about the information passed on to the author by the "Ascended Masters," and which you confirmed when I pressed you in one of my spiritual healing sessions. You said this book "poisoned the mind."

I made a negative comment about this book that I regret making, because you told me to be careful about how I talked about this book, and this automatically put the lady on the defensive; but it did initiate a conversation, and we ended up exchanging our newly published books; she gave me a copy of her book *The Gifts of Responsibility,* and I gave her a copy of my book *Keeper of the Flame* that I had on consignment in the store.

Now tell me what you think of this, Padre. I honestly believe Providence had us meet and exchange our books because we both have something to learn from each other. She will get something from *Keeper of the Flame* that she needs, and I will get something from *The Gifts of Responsibility* that I need—and which I am getting in fact because I'm half way through her book and I love what I've read so far.

Last night as I was going to sleep I got an image of being in the womb of her soul. Her book is the story of how she expanded her Roman Catholic faith to include what can simply be called a New Age spiritual perspective on life, and the impression that her book made upon me was translated into the image of being in the womb of her soul; which told me that she's in the process of creating her own spiritual identity; and the next stage of her journey is to give birth to her spiritual self!

She's a hound of heaven that has been clasped by the Hand of God and will not rest until she gives birth to her spiritual self; and I was a hound of heaven that was clasped by the Hand of God and gave birth to my spiritual self. As I wrote in *Keeper of the Flame,* I gave birth to my spiritual self in my mother's kitchen while she was kneading bread dough on the kitchen table; so I think Providence had us meet because we have something for each other. What that would be, I don't know; but I believe this to be so.

And I think she would agree with this, because this is what she wrote in *The Gifts of Responsibility*: "There are no coincidences, only synchronicity. Once we have understood and mastered this cosmic phenomenon (karma), life will no longer be perceived as a struggle. The possibilities of unending adventures comprised of many moments in time will appear as part of a cosmic reality we can refer to as *Divine Orchestration*" (p. 5).

So, Padre; I know that you orchestrated our meeting, because she's a Roman Catholic who expanded her faith to include the many dimensions of spirituality, as I have done, and we have something to learn from each other; and I thank you for bringing us together. But to get back to the point of this letter; what exactly defines a hound of heaven?

When you said "I want to inebriate myself with pain," I understood exactly what you meant because that resonated with me; but to explain this would be like trying to explain the color blue to a person born blind. It can't be done; which is why my mentor Gurdjieff said that there is only self-initiation into the mysteries of life. Nonetheless I will try to come to an understanding by way of analogy. Take a person who is addicted. He cannot help himself. He has to have his fix, be it alcohol, drugs, cigarettes, sex, or whatever. In like manner, a hound of heaven has to have his fix also, which is God.

A hound of heaven craves God, and he will get his God fix wherever he can, which is why Francis Thompson calls him a hound of heaven. Like the hound that has caught the scent of God, he will not rest until he finds God. "Rise, clasp My hand, and come!" says God, and the hound of heaven has no choice but to come to God!

When a soul is called by God, it becomes a seeker—or, as the poet calls him, a hound of heaven. This is why you wanted to inebriate yourself with pain—because in your pain you sacrificed yourself for Jesus, and in your sacrifice you got your God fix; which in one of my healing sessions you called your "glory." I understood that, Padre.

The woman who channeled you didn't understand, because she was not addicted to God like we were; but in our addiction to God we separated ourselves from the rest of the world. This is why you said to me, "We are very much alike."

You got your God fix through self-sacrifice, and I got my God fix by "working" on myself as I lived the Way. I had to be very resourceful to feed my habit, but I became so frantic when I couldn't get enough of God that I fell for that offshoot Christian solar cult teaching that promised the Logos with the solar techniques. I was so desperate for my God fix that I didn't care if this was true or not, and I enrolled in this teaching and practiced the solar techniques for three years when I began to feel the effects on my eyes. I went to an ophthalmologist, and the rest is history; which I may write about in a story one day.

I have a feeling that you want me to write this story, don't you? That's why I thought about an early draft of *The Sunworshipper* the other day; but we can talk about this some other time. The point I wanted to make with this letter is that unless one is called by God he will never understand what it means to be a hound of heaven.

That's all I have to say for now, except that I have a dentist appointment at noon and would like you to accompany me because I dread going to the dentist.

I remain,
Your faithful companion,
Orest

12. OREST WALKS WITH OREST

Letters to Ascended Master
St. Padre Pio,
Monday, August 15, 2011
6: 30 A. M.

Dear Padre,

Sitting at my writing desk, I can look out the window to my left that looks onto the main stretch of our street and yesterday morning as I was writing I turned to look out and saw Orest walking very slowly towards our house.

I got up to check and make sure it was Orest, and it was; so I got dressed (I had on a pair of shorts and T shirt, which I always wear in the summer when I'm writing), and went out to the front deck and yelled to Orest in Italian: *"Bon jorno, Oresto! Aspeta!"*

I went upstairs and woke Penny up to let her know where I would be. "I'm going for a walk with Orest," I said, and laughed.

Orest is a friend of Eugenio, who has a cottage just down the street that he comes to half a dozen times a summer, and Orest and his wife had come up for a visit and he was out for an early morning walk. When I saw him walking down the street I just had to go for a walk with him because it was a coincidence fraught with so much symbolic meaning that I would never forgive myself if I didn't go for a walk with him.

The chances of going for a walk with a man called Orest were astronomical. In fact, Orest S. (his surname even has the same initial as mine, and our street is called STOCCO CIRCLE, the same as my surname) was the only man I had ever met with the same name as mine, so I knew that this was divinely orchestrated. So, Padre; I know that you planned my walk with Orest yesterday morning, and now I have to explore the reason why...

Penny came into my room for her morning coffee and chat this morning, as she always does, so I had to put my letter to you aside; and then I had to do my morning chores (today is garbage day, and I had to take out the garbage and blue boxes for recycling), and after I fed all the critters—our goldfish, cat, and seeds and peanuts for our outdoor critters—I was free to continue with this letter.

Over coffee Penny and I were talking about my writing. She felt that I quoted too much. "Good God," she said, "you should be confident in your own voice by now. I just think that all those quotes get in the way. I feel like you keep grinding your point, and I come away exhausted. I love your writing, but it's exhausting. That's what my sister said about your novel *My Unborn Child.* She said the novel kept calling her, but it exhausted her. You don't want to exhaust your reader. You want them to walk away feeling inspired. I think you should just write with your own voice. You don't need all those quotes."

She's right. And this is what you tried to tell me Sunday morning when I felt compelled to go for a walk with Orest.

I listened to Orest talk about his life, and it was so engaging that it took two and a half hours to walk around Stocco Circle, which normally takes less than ten minutes; and after talking with Penny this morning I think I finally got the point—that my life is no less interesting than Orest's life (he was born in Calabria, Italy where I was born, and he immigrated with his young family to Canada because destiny called him), and I don't need to lean upon other authors to validate the integrity of my own life and voice.

And this, believe it or not, is exactly what a psychic told me several months before *My Unborn Child* was published last summer. She was at Mountainview Mall in Midland, and she gave me a reading (twenty minutes for sixty dollars), and told me that I should just write about my own life, tell my own story, that I shouldn't quote all those authors that I like to quote because they just got in the way of my story. "The story of your life is going to be your most successful book," she said.

So there you have it, Padre; but it wasn't until Orest went for a walk with Orest yesterday morning that I finally got the point! But what was it about Orest's life that fascinated me?

If I had to distill his life story, I would say it was his integrity that defined him. It was obvious from the many anecdotes of his working life that he shared with me that he hates cheaters, liars, and hypocrites (he told me he was Catholic but didn't go to church because of his experiences with priests), and I related to everything he said; perhaps that's why you orchestrated our walk yesterday morning— to set me free to write about my own life without depending upon other authors and let my life speak for itself.

But did you have to orchestrate a walk with another Orest born in the same part of Italy as me and with a defining steely integrity for me to see myself in him and learn to trust in the integrity of my own life and voice?

I don't know what to think, Padre; especially since I lashed out at you Friday afternoon when I came out of the dentist's office with one less tooth that made me so self-conscious that my vanity almost kept me away from my spiritual book discussion class in Orillia the following day. God, was I angry!

"Thank you, Padre!" I lashed out at you in disgust as I drove home from my dentist appointment. I never thought I would lose my tooth. I thought the worst scenario would be a root canal, but the crack from the cherry pit that I bit into was too deep and it had to be extracted and it shows when I smile!

Now I have to get a partial plate because it's much too expensive to get bridgework (three thousand dollars). Even a plate is an expense we don't need at this time. We just got news that the bearings on our lawn tractor deck were ceased and have to be replaced, plus a new belt, which is another expense we can't afford at this time, not to mention the expense for the muffler on my van this week. I was not happy when I came out of the dentist's office, and I don't know how I was able to manage my anger as I did. I wanted to scream, but all I could say was *"Old whore life" sure screwed me this week!"*

I have to stop writing. I'm still too angry.

I remain,
Not a very happy camper,
Orest

13. EVERY CHERRY HAS A PIT

Letters to Ascended Master
St. Padre Pio,
Tuesday, August 16, 2011
5:35 A. M.

Dear Padre,

It's going to take some time before I calm down. It may not seem like much a year or two from now, but losing a tooth for something as accidental as biting into a cherry pit has really got me worked up. It's the straw that broke the camel's back!

What really hurts is that I asked you to accompany me to my dentist appointment, hoping you would work a miracle and let me walk out of the dentist's office with my dignity intact; but no, I lost a tooth that's so obvious I've stopped smiling.

I have to get a partial plate because we can't afford the expense of an implant or bridgework (four to five thousand dollars for an implant, and three thousand for bridgework). Maybe down the road, if one of my novels connects with the public and we can afford such luxuries as proper dental care, I will get bridgework done; but for now I have to get a partial plate because I have to salvage my dignity somehow.

And to think that a little thing like a cherry pit could cause so much personal devastation? Talk about a journey through vanity to humility! That damn cherry pit has initiated a chain of events that I could have done without, and I have to ask why?

When Penny and I went out for a Tim Hortons coffee last night I thought of Jesus cursing the barren fig tree. *"That damn cherry pit!"* I exploded. *"I'm not going to attend any more classes at that woman's house!"*

I don't know why yet, but I cannot go back to the house where I bit into the cherry pit after one of our Spiritual Discourse classes. I can't make the connection yet, Padre; but there's a message in the barren fig tree and the little bowl of cherries that the woman who hosted the classes put out for after-class fellowship.

I don't want to give up our classes, but I'm so angry at the loss of my tooth that I just can't bring myself to go back to that woman's house anymore; and it's not simply a matter of vanity. It's much deeper than that. I can't put my finger on it, but it has to do with the clash of my energies and "old whore life." I rankle the "old whore," and she stirs up karma!

It has puzzled the world why Jesus cursed the fig tree, but I think I understand why Jesus did it. I think he could see "old whore life"—those negative forces that resisted him every step of the way—and that day he had enough and cursed the barren fig tree. *"Let no fruit grow on thee henceforward for ever,"* said Jesus (Math. 21: 19).

That's how I feel about the cherry pit that cracked my tooth and gave me so much aggravation that I cursed the cherry pit like Jesus cursed the barren fig tree. It may be a preposterous comparison, but I don't think so. There's a connection between the barren fig tree that could not nourish Jesus when he was hungry and the cherry pit that caused me so much aggravation, and I think the connection has to do with how my energies clash with the energies of "old whore life." But that's too deep to ponder now.

"Thank you, Padre!" I lashed out at you when I came out of the dentist's office Friday afternoon—as if you had anything to do with my cracked tooth!

Or did you? Was Spirit orchestrating the next chapter of my life? Was Spirit telling me that I bit too hard on life with my spiritual musings on "old whore life" (now published as *Old Whore Life: Exploring the Shadow Side of Karma*) and struck a nerve—like I did when I bit too hard on the cherry pit and struck a nerve? Have I seen through life's bowl of cherries and gone straight to the pits of life?

The saying "life is a bowl of cherries" has taken on a whole new meaning for me, because I *know* now that every cherry has a pit; which is what my spiritual musings on "old whore life" are all about—*the cherry pits of life!*

What gets me is how innocent it all was. When I told my dentist what happened to my tooth, he said, "Life is full of surprises," and was I surprised when it happened!

We were having fellowship after our class. I placed three cherries onto my plate along with a piece of cinnamon cake that Penny and I brought, and after I ate the cherries I picked up the piece of cake and took a bite, but I hadn't noticed that a cherry pit had stuck to the bottom of the cake and I bit into it and yelped in pain when it struck a nerve.

I didn't know I had cracked my tooth, so I didn't go to the dentist right away. I thought the pain would eventually go away, but after two weeks of chewing on the other side of my mouth I went to the dentist and learned that my tooth couldn't be saved.

So what's the karmic lesson? Is there a price to pay for the cake we eat? Is this what it means when we say that we can't have our cake and eat it too? We all know that nothing is for nothing in this world, so what's the lesson, Padre?

Life may very well be a bowl of cherries, but every cherry has a pit! Is that the lesson? I really don't have much more to say. I'm in a real funk, and I don't know when I'm going to get out of it. It may take a few days, weeks, or months even; but I had to write this letter because I just had to vent. Thanks for listening.

I remain,
Still not a happy camper,
Orest

14. THE TEMPEST HAS PASSED

Letters to Ascended Master
St. Padre Pio,
Thursday, August 18, 2011
6: 30 A. M.

Dear Padre,

The tempest has passed. I've calmed down somewhat. I'm still not a happy camper, but I'm beginning to adjust to my new reality. I haven't made my appointment with the denturist recommended by my dentist. I'm not ready yet. I'm not that resolved.

I drove Penny to Barrie yesterday morning to catch the 7 o'clock Go Train to Toronto. She flew to Thunder Bay for her niece's wedding, and when I came home I went for a walk around our street.

I brought my notebook with me. I felt that the tempest of my dismay had passed, and I jotted that down. As I'm walking, I find myself crossing the street to walk on the other side. I have my head down, thinking about the foul karmic wind that blew into my life and threw me out of spiritual balance when I spotted a ten-dollar bill on the ground.

"What's this?" I wondered, with mixed emotions. I wondered who had lost it, knowing that there was no way I could return it to the person, which gave me moral permission to keep it; and I knew it was a sign that pointed to something beyond itself. When something out of the ordinary happens, I've learned that it points to something else; in other words, Spirit is trying to tell us something—but what?

I knew it was a good sign, but I was much too suspicious of good signs to read too much into it, so I resisted the temptation…

Penny just called to say good morning, so I had to suspend my letter; she had some good news to share. She brought her father to the casino last night. He went on his motorized scooter and she walked because the casino is a short distance from her father's apartment, and her two sisters joined them. Penny told me she won four hundred and fifty dollars; and then she shared the dream she had last night, and one part of her dream had to do with a phone call she got from an investment lawyer from New York!

So, Padre; is Spirit teasing us again? We've gotten so many signs that my writing is going to connect that we're both very suspicious of good signs, and we refuse to read into them what we desperately wish for; that's why I said to Penny when she shared her dream, "I'm not going there," meaning that I wasn't going to tease myself again.

See what "old whore life" has done to me? She's made me suspicious of the language of life, and it's going to take time to regain my confidence. Not that I doubt Spirit's guidance, which would be foolish; but both Penny and I are tired of grasping at hope.

Padre, you were known as "a man of hope and prayer" in your life; maybe you could shed some light on our situation. Is Spirit teasing us with these signs and symbols, or are we just teasing ourselves by wanting them to mean what we would like them to mean; or, do they really point there, to a comfortable, successful future?

I have a little job to go to today, a few hours of taping a washroom for a contractor whom I work for now and then, and Sunday I went to see an old customer of mine (I taped the drywall of his new house before my bypass surgery) to give him a price for taping their basement, so if I get this job it will offset some of these expenses that the foul karmic wind has blown into my life—and by calling it a foul karmic wind I mean that I didn't see it coming, and the surprise really upset me.

I would love nothing more than to be free to write without the worry of monthly expenses; that's why we've always read the signs and symbols the way we have, which upon first appearance point to where we would like to be; but we've grown suspicious, because life is crowding us.

I don't want to go into detail about these signs and symbols, because there are too many; but not only do we get signs and symbols, I've been told outright by you and other Spiritual Masters that we're headed where the signs and symbols point to.

When I asked you point blank in one of my sessions if my writing was going to pay off you said, "He will get what he seeks." This wasn't clear enough for the woman who channeled you, so she asked if this meant financial remuneration, and you said yes. And at one of my book discussion classes recently a member of the class, who is also a spiritual sensitive who gives me information that Spiritual Masters pass on to her about my writing, said they told her to tell me to remember where I came from, who I am, and where I am going—implying that when my books connect it's going to change my life financially and socially. So, what am I to think, Padre?

I don't know, and quite frankly in the mood I'm in after this last little tempest I really don't give a damn. I'm just going to plug along as I've always done and hope for the best. You see, I too am a man of hope! Maybe not a man of prayer like you (you prayed the rosary dozens of times a day, calling the rosary your "weapon"), but I have to have hope to get me through the rest of this life; otherwise I'd have to resign myself to a life of angry desperation—which is a side of life that Thoreau failed to acknowledge when he said that the vast majority of mankind has resigned itself to a life of "quiet desperation."

I know, I know; it's all about surrender. We have to let go and let God. I know this, but what the hell's the point of evolving through millions of lifetimes only to realize our own individuality—a new "I" of God that we have to surrender to God? Isn't that like saying that God has to surrender to God to become more God? *It is a mystery!*

We touched on this theme in one of my spiritual healing sessions in our discussion on the selfless self. I guess I still have a long way to go before I experience that bliss that you experienced when you crossed over—that joyous surrender that lifted you to the heights of Ascended Spiritual Master.

You'll have to share more of that experience with me when I start my next project with you after I publish *Healing with Padre Pio*—unless, of course, you choose to tell me in a dream. I'd love that. But, as I said, Spirit does what Spirit wills, so I'm not going to hang my hat on that dream!

Your tempered companion,
Orest

15. WHY BOTHER?

Letter to Ascended Master
St. Padre Pio,
Friday, August 19, 2011
6: 50 A. M.

Dear Padre,

You did tell me after the spiritual healing you gave me that I would write more from the heart now than from the mind, which you said would be how I would connect with my reader, but whether what I write is from the heart or mind I have to ask you—something that has been brewing from the day those foul karmic winds began to blow into my life, leading to the unexpected loss of my tooth and leaving me in a state of inner turmoil—a very pertinent question: *why bother?*

I've devoted the best energies of my life to finding my true self, and I was blessed to awaken to the Way—the mysterious River of God that flows through life that you also awakened to by living *la via di sofferenza* (which is why we have a meeting of minds)—and I devoted my best creative energies to demystifying the Way for my reader with every book that I write; but I ask you again: *why bother?*

When you were alive you devoted every ounce of your energy to serving Jesus in his mission to bring souls back home to God, saying your daily Mass which people came from everywhere to witness, such the spiritual intensity of your Masses, and listening to over one hundred confessions daily (people were given numbers, there were so many who wanted to confess their sins to you, and it has been estimated that you heard up to five million confessions in your lifetime), and still you prayed to do more for the love of Jesus and your fellow man—which you did by initiating the project of a new hospital which you called a House for the Relief of Suffering—and still you wanted to do more because your love to serve was so great that you could never do enough; but I can't help but ask the question: *why bother?*

The more I experience life—what I witness on the daily news and life around me—the more I am forced to agree with what the great Spiritual Master Rebazar Tarzs said to Paul Twitchell: "As you grow older in your observations of the peoples of the Earth world, it becomes more noticeable that stupidity is the reigning virtue."

In principle, I know you would agree with this comment; but having experienced you for an hour and a half once a month for ten months I know that you would also say, "Yes, that's one interpretation." And then you would proceed to inform me of the goodness of man, which would then soften my hardened and inflexible view and pry my heart open a little more; but you know what, Padre? I really don't know why I should bother.

You saw results from your service to Jesus and your fellow man—despite all the flak that you got from those who resented your spiritual grace—by the love and affection of your "spiritual family," but my world is barren of this goodness that comes with service. Which can mean one of two things: either my heart is not pure, or my time has not yet come.

Let's look at the first. Is my heart pure in my intent? I've always wanted to write, and I write about my life experiences—with a liberal use of the imagination; but do I write for myself, or to serve my fellow man by passing on the wisdom of my spiritual quest?

In all honesty the very thought offends me that I am writing for pure selfish reasons, because I vowed that I would pass on the wisdom of my own spiritual quest simply because I KNOW how hard it is to find the Way and I simply want to make the search easier for the seeker. That's the *raison d'être* of my writing life—to help the seeker awaken to the Way; but I cannot help but wonder: *why bother?*

I've experienced this feeling before, Padre. In fact, "old whore life" pushed me to the point once where I climbed on my platform and shouted: *"Let the world find its own way!"* And ironically you confirmed this when you told me that "life is a journey of the self." If life is an individual journey, then *why bother?*

Everyone has to find their own way through the labyrinthine tunnels of their own karma; and we can give them all the Ariadne's string in the world, but it won't mean a damn thing—because "life is a journey of the self." So again I ask: *why bother?*

I read a book a couple of weeks ago about a Roman Catholic who could no longer suffer the indignities of her faith—the same indignities that I suffered in my belief of eternal damnation and that salvation was only possible through Jesus Christ and the "one true Church"—and I experienced this author's spiritual anguish as she wrestled her soul free from these fatuous doctrines, which only goes to prove your truth that "life is a journey of the self," and I have done everything in my power—which I'm still doing with these letters to you—to awaken my reader to the eternally saving grace of the Way, which is everywhere to be found; but again I ask, *why bother?*—because no one's listening!

You told me it would take three years for the ripple effect of my writing to reach out and touch the people who would hear what I have to say, and it's only been a little over one year now since you told me this; so, am I impatient? And why should I believe you? Am I supposed to have blind faith in you?

I know you did everything you could to bolster my confidence by showing my yet-to-be published books to my spiritual sensitive, and that I should commit myself to getting them out (especially my novel on Jesus, which my spiritual sensitive felt was the main reason why I was having those spiritual healing sessions—to motivate me to get *Jesus Wears Dockers, The Gospel Conspiracy Story* published), but since that foul karmic wind blew into my life I can't help but ask: *why bother?*

Last night, sleeping alone in our big king size bed because Penny went up north to attend her niece's wedding, I almost came to tears because I could have poured more energy into making Penny's life a little more financially secure, and I had to ask myself whether all of my creative efforts to demystify the Way were worth it.

I broke the code of the sayings of Jesus, which is why you want to see my Jesus novel out there, but why bother Padre? You told me that a little worry is good, that it keeps one sharp and on edge; but I tell you that the anxiety wrought by the struggle to survive with dignity is not worth the bother of the commitment to serve life—and yet, I know it has to be this way because service is the ultimate goal of life. *God, what a conundrum!*

But I do have one reader who loves my writing and believes in me, and you can guess who that is—Penny Lynn, the love of my life; and thank God for her belief in me or I would have given up long ago. If it weren't for her I wouldn't have *My Unborn Child* and *Keeper of the Flame* out there patiently seeking to find their readers. They may not have connected yet, but at least they're out there; and that's all that matters.

I guess when all is said and done (I'm through with all this moaning and groaning) I have to just bow my head and keep butting at life until I either smash my skull or break through to the other side where all the karmic rewards for my service to life are waiting for me. What did Henley say in his poem *Invictus*?

"In the fell clutch of circumstance
    I have not winced nor cried aloud.
Under the bludgeonings of chance
    My head is bloody, but unbowed."

I guess what it comes down to is that these foul karmic winds ("the fell clutch of circumstance") are bound to blow through our life every so often because our journey is all about spiritual resolution; so we really have no choice but to hold our course through the tempests. But I don't mind confessing, Padre; it can get quite fatiguing!

I remain,
A very tired companion,
Orest

16. THE STRAW THAT BROKE THE CAMEL'S BACK

Letters to Ascended Master
St. Padre Pio,
Wednesday, August 24, 2011
5: 39 A. M.

Dear Padre,

I fell off the tightrope, and I'm too ashamed to talk about it; but I have to tell you that I'm still in a state of anger because of my tooth. Well, not just my tooth; that was the straw that broke the camel's back.

I didn't think I had that kind of anger still left in me since you cured my wounded Christian soul. I harbored a deep anger for my Roman Catholic faith, which is why you came into my life. My spiritual guide arranged for me to meet you through the sensitive who channeled you so we could work together; but first you had to heal me of my anger, which you did because I no longer feel as I did about Christianity, but ever since I bit into that cherry pit and lost my tooth I've been unbelievably angry.

I came close to the source of my anger in my last spiritual musing ("The Foul Winds of Life"), which has to do with my character flaw of faultfinding; but even though I've raised this flaw to a conscious level I'm still in a state of bitter anger. That's why I fell off the tightrope. It's not an excuse, but I just didn't give a damn about my life, and I fell into the bowels of my own mind and forfeited myself to fantasies that gave me temporary relief from life. It was foolish, but I just didn't give a damn and let go. Now I know how an alcoholics feel, or drug addicts; they just let go and give in because they have to escape from the pressures of their life.

It may be a small thing, biting into a cherry pit and losing a perfectly good tooth; but that was the straw that broke the camel's back. The real issue is all of the other straws that the good camel had to carry before that final straw broke its back. That final straw symbolizes the full brunt of one's life-load. And just what is my life-load?

In a word, my unbelievable struggle to find my true self. I had to find the Way, which was a monumental task; and when I found the Way I had to live it, because that was the only way I could find my true self. To put it bluntly, one does not find their true self, one BECOMES their true self by living the Way. And then writing about my search so I could pass on my quest to other seekers. This has tried my soul.

Unless one has been called by God to find their true self they will never understand how demanding it is to be a spiritual seeker, let alone write about the quest; and when I bit into that damn cherry pit last month that caused me to lose my tooth I was so angry that I cursed the cherry pit because I felt let down just as Jesus was let down by the barren fig tree, and in my state of anger I fell into a state of wicked despair.

I called my despair a "life funk" to make light of it to Penny and our friends, but it was and still is much more than a funk. I feel like I was put into the forge of life (my private hell) to be tempered some more when I had no desire to be tempered; I just wanted some respite from life, that's all. Given all on my efforts, I felt I deserved respite.

Padre, I remember from your letters to your Spiritual Director how despaired you were at certain times in your life, how your soul cried out in anguish and your only recourse was more prayer; but I'm not the praying type. My context is different from yours. I know that I am the author of my own state of consciousness, and my anger comes from some of the choices that I have made in my life that were blindly stupid. I'm angry with myself. I don't blame anyone for my despair. I cursed the cherry pit because it brought everything to a head, which was too much for me to bear, and I lost it. So, what do I do now?

Forgive myself? Is that what I heard you say to me in the quiet of my mind?

Forgive yourself, and then love yourself, because you cannot love yourself until you are free of the guilt that makes you angry.

And how do I forgive myself of all that blind stupidity? Have you any idea of how stupid I've been in some of my decisions?

You are not alone in the gifts of stupidity, my son. But you are more than the sum of your stupid decisions. Remember what I told you, that it's all about understanding. Well, now you know that you have made stupid decisions in your life, and it's time to forgive yourself.

How? How can I forgive myself when the memories of my stupidities haunt me practically every hour of every day? I can't get past them. They rise up to torment me as I work, as I drive, as I watch TV, as I read, as I eat, and especially when I'm trying to sleep; everything that I do is a link to one stupid decision or another, and I can't free myself of my stupid self; so how can I forgive myself? It's easier said than done!

I know. That was my dilemma as well. I prayed, and you write to ease your pain and guilt. Well, write yourself through your guilt. Use your pain for your writing. Let writing be your saving grace. As you said, your context is different; that's why life is a journey of the self. Think about it.

To be honest Padre, I've been toying with the idea of writing a book of stories, with the title "We May Be Tiny, But We're Not Small." The other two stories would be "The Cherry Pit" and "La Famiglia." These stories would force me to deal with the guilt of some of my stupid decisions—not to mention another book of stories under the title "The Sunworshipper" which would deal with the enormous guilt of my stupid decision to practice solar techniques that did irreparable damage to my eyes. I'm reminded every day of the enormous stupidity of that decision, and I don't know if I can ever forgive myself.

That's why you have to write about it. By writing about it you will work your way through your guilt, and I promise that you will find yourself on the other side free of the pain of your despair. I will guide you through your pain. I promise to be there for you.

Forgive myself? That's the new challenge of my life. I've never given this concept of self-forgiveness much thought. Is that because I was much too self-centered to confront my own stupidity?

Your quest kept you so busy that you had no time or energy to pour into self-pity. Now that you have realized your spiritual goal, you have to deal with the consciousness of your self-guilt. As you say, that's your new challenge now. Don't despair. You have plenty of time to see this through.

About falling off the tightrope?

What about it? Is it so hard to admit that you are human? You are in the flesh, and when soul is in the flesh it will always seek the pleasures of the flesh. It is a fact of life. Accept it, and try harder next time. As they say today, don't beat yourself up over it. Tomorrow's another day.

What about my anger?

It will wear thin soon enough. You are not a man to stay angry very long. It is not in your make-up. You are what you are, and be proud of it. Soon you will be caught up in your new challenge, and all of the universe will conspire to assist you.

Fair enough. Thank you, Padre. I didn't expect this at all this morning. You are full of surprises. I don't know what else to say. I feel like I've just been given a new set of marching orders!

I remain,
Your humble companion,
Orest

17. STUPIDITY IS NOT A GIFT OF GOD

Letters to Ascended Master
St. Padre Pio,
Thursday, August 25, 2011
6:06 A. M.

Dear Padre,

"'Nature patterns after man, not man after nature,' said Phylos the Tibetan," which I quoted at our spiritual contemplation class in Barrie last Sunday to make the point that man's consciousness is responsible for many of our climatic catastrophes. "Nature is trying to wake us up to our responsibility to life with all these natural disasters, but man is too stupid to see it," I added, and then referenced Rebazar Tarzs who said that the more experience one has with the peoples of the world, the more they will see that stupidity is the reigning virtue. And I couldn't agree more, because I'm as guilty as the next person of this monumental human defect!

I should tell you Padre, I began writing the first story in my new literary endeavor. I started writing "La Famiglia." And I also wrote the introduction to the book of stories, which I may keep or not; it all depends upon how the stories turn out. But I have to tell you, I'm terrified of going where I know these stories are going to take me.

I have to confront some of the stupid decisions that I made in my life to extricate myself of the guilt that haunts me. As you said, how can I love myself when I have all this guilt that makes me angry with myself? And I thought I had dealt with my anger issue in my spiritual healing sessions with you! Obviously, I'm not yet finished with this issue of anger; and I don't think I will be until I work through my guilt in my stories.

So, Padre, what do you say I open up this subject of man's stupidity? I've come to the realization that the more conscious we become of how karma works, the more clearly we will see the relationship between cause and effect; and human stupidity comes into play when man sees this relationship and refuses to change his life.

For example, science has proven that smoking causes lung cancer; but people continue to smoke knowing full well what might happen. Many do it because it's a very difficult habit to break, which only creates what has been appropriately called "guilty pleasure," and others simply toss the dice, taking the risk that they won't get cancer from smoking, and the more stubborn ones go into denial and refuse to see the connection between smoking and lung cancer. These people are deceiving themselves.

What about the battered housewife who refuses to get help because she does not want the world to know her situation? She's too proud to admit that her husband beats her. Is that stupidity, or what? Pride is born of vanity, and vanity is responsible for many stupid decisions. My vanity was responsible for many of my stupid decisions. God, when I think back on my life I want to throw up at how stupid I was because of my vanity! But as you said, I shouldn't beat myself up over it now; tomorrow's another day.

"If I had children, the one gift that I would love to pass on to them would be the gift of spontaneity," I said to Penny yesterday, because this gift would free my child from the fear of taking risks. Vanity and fear. They were my constant companions.

I don't know where I'm going with this. I think what I want to say is that **stupidity is not a gift of God; it's entirely man made**. We know that pollution has devastating environmental consequences, but we continue to spew toxic gases into the atmosphere; and we destroy our soil with chemical fertilizers that contain phosphorus that runs off into the lakes that feeds the algae that kill the lakes; and we poison our animal food supply with chemicals, our chickens, pigs, and cattle whose waste also contains phosphorus. Is this stupid, or what? It's no wonder the Spiritual Hierarchy has decided to intervene to help save the planet from man's unstoppable march of stupidity.

I'm right, aren't I? There's a great spiritual intervention going on as I write this letter, isn't there? This is what we've been told by the Nine Enlightened Ones in the book *The Only Planet of Choice*. And this is what you confirmed in my spiritual healing sessions. So, what's the antidote for man's compulsive stupidity?

I know the answer to this question. We have to raise the spiritual consciousness of the world; right? And how do we do that?

In your own way; each according to their own means, and all in light of their love for man by taking responsibility for their own life.

That's the thought I just got from you; but I don't want to pursue this mode of communication. I'm not comfortable enough yet with this process, because I don't trust my mind to be free of its own agenda; so if you don't mind, Padre, I'll just try to reason it out on my own and follow my nudges and insights as I'm accustomed to doing.

It appears then that man's capacities for stupidity has become an incorrigible habit, and we all know how difficult habits are to break; but raising the level of the spiritual consciousness of the world will only work when it reaches the tipping point and man makes a shift from ego-driven behavior to soul-driven behavior. Is this possible, Padre?

This is the challenge, isn't it? I guess all we can do is play our little part in this BIG GAME OF LIFE, and hope for the best.

In Spirit,
Your faithful companion,
Orest

18. MAYBE WHEN THE SNOW FLIES

Letters to Ascended Master
St. Padre Pio,
Friday, August 26, 2011
6:10 A. M.

Dear Padre,

I'm almost ready to go back to work on *Healing with Padre Pio.* I have the last chapter to write, but I want to read the whole manuscript before I bring my novel to closure. I'm going to edit as I read. I want to pare it down as much as I can because it's a long book and people today don't have patience for long books. They like short books like *Tuesdays with Morrie,* by Mitch Albom; or *The Alchemist,* by Paulo Coelho; or *Heaven is for Real,* by Todd Burpo (all of which I loved by the way); anything up to two hundred pages, but not much longer. It's a hurried culture, and nobody has time to read big books.

It seems like the dust from this last tempest of my life is starting to settle, because I don't feel like raging at the world. I'm still angry, but I feel like my anger is burning itself out; and I can't wait for it to go out entirely because that's not a nice place to be. I can't imagine what it would be like to be angry all the time, but I'm sure some people are.

Living in a constant state of anger would be nothing short of hell. One would never be open to the joy, beauty, and goodness of life. One would be in a constant state of denial of anything that would threaten their anger. That's how I felt in the heat of my anger. I didn't want it to stop. I wanted to rage at life, because it felt good. I enjoyed being angry. I felt justified in my anger, despite my self-awareness. I knew that I had invited the tempest into my life by my own karma, but I just had to vent; and I found scriptural justification for venting in Jesus Christ's cursing of the barren fig tree.

I'm going to ask you about this in our next project. I want to know why Jesus cursed the fig tree. I honestly feel that he was fed up. The fig tree was the last straw. It let Jesus down, and he had had enough; so he cursed the fig tree for not having what it should have had—figs. So, why was that fig tree barren when it should have been full of fresh ripe figs? That's the real question, isn't it?

I don't know the answer, but I understand why Jesus cursed the fig tree. I can't explain how he felt, because this goes to a state of being that can't be put to words. It speaks to Christ's human nature. Jesus was disappointed that the fig tree was barren, and it was like he said to the fig tree: *you choose to be barren, and barren you shall be forever!*

It's like Jesus was aware of the genetic predisposition of life, and when he saw that the fig tree was not true to its own genetic purpose, which was to produce fruit, he simply confirmed the barren fig tree's choice to stay barren. Again, it's like he said to the fig tree: *you have chosen to go against your own nature, now live with your choice!*

Was this Christ's way of telling us that the purpose of life is to bear fruit—whatever that fruit may be? I'd sure like to know what you have to say about this, Padre. I can't take this thought any further now, so I'm going to move on to something else.

I don't know when I'm going to do it, but I want to write to you on the subject of sin, confession, damnation, the one-life theory that Christians believe in, and the real meaning of Christ's crucifixion, plus a few other topics that need to be aired. I want to bring some clarity to these subjects that we touched upon in *Healing with Padre Pio.*

Now that I think about it, you gave me a lot to think about; didn't you? I'm only now beginning to see how much you have given me; but I'm having second thoughts about publishing these letters in a blog. I don't think it's a question of getting cold feet. I think it's the effect of that last tempest in my life. It knocked the heart out of me. Penny caught my emotions precisely when she said: "You're disappointed because you haven't realized your dreams yet, that's why you're angry."

I don't disagree with her. Writing is a difficult life, and few writers can make a living off their writing. It can get very disheartening. But we're driven to write; so what are we to do? Get angry? Every once in a while we have to vent, and that damn cherry pit gave me all the reason I needed to get all that pent-up rage out of my system. It's not all out yet. And it won't be out until I write my book of stories; and perhaps another book of stories that will deal with the guilt of my involvement with that wicked solar cult teaching.

I see this new challenge as a demanding new chapter in my life, and I have mixed feelings about it. I want to take it on, but I'm afraid to go there because I don't want to relive those emotions; and yet I have to work my way through them to absolve myself of the guilt of my stupid decisions, don't I? That's what you suggested I do.

I'm reminded of a letter that my literary mentor Ernest "Papa" Hemingway wrote to his friend and writer F. Scott Fitzgerald: "Forget your personal tragedy. We are all bitched from the start and you especially have to be hurt like hell before you can write seriously. But when you get the damned hurt use it—don't cheat with it. Be as faithful to it as a scientist—but don't think anything is of any importance because it happens to you or anyone belonging to you" (*Selected Letters*, p. 408).

Hemingway inspires me to take on my new literary challenge, but I can't say when I will dive into it. Maybe when the snow flies...

In Spirit,
Your faithful companion,
Orest

19. WHEN PUSH COMES TO SHOVE

Letters to Ascended Master
St. Padre Pio,
Saturday, August 27, 2011
8:40 A. M.

Dear Padre,

What to do? That's the question...

Do what you are supposed to do, and let God take care of the rest, I hear you say in the quiet of my mind; which I know is the right thing to do, whether you inspired this thought or not because I have responsibilities that have to be taken care of and which I'm perfectly capable of doing. I can't take on big jobs because of my health, but I can certainly pace myself with smaller jobs and fulfill my obligations to Penny, to our life, and to myself; but I pour my best energies into my writing.

I have to shift priorities. I have to realign my life to be in sync with the totality of my life and not allot so much energy to writing and then use that as an excuse to shirk my responsibilities to Penny; so why not start today?

Padre, I have to do something to avert the possibility of selling our new home here and moving back up north into our triplex; but the expenses of maintaining two houses (the mortgage on our triplex and taxes and insurance on two homes are killing us), may force us to do just that within the next two or three years. I have to come up with a game plan.

I'm going to try to get more work. That's the only solution. I can't do big jobs anymore, like taping and painting a whole house; but I can take on smaller jobs, which I feel is the only way out of our conundrum. I certainly can't depend on one of my books connecting with the public, despite what you said about the ripple effect taking place within three years of my sessions with you. I can't trust that process, thank you very much.

Does this mean I don't trust God? No; not as such. "Trust Allah, but tie up your camel," say the Sufis. I have to trust what I know can work, and that's to go out and get work so we don't have to sell our beautiful home in Georgian Bay.

You know I don't want to do this, but when push comes to shove a man has to do what he has to do; and even though it may not be a push at this moment, I can feel that the push may very well become a shove in a few years, and then I'll go into panic mode.

So, Padre; what do you say? Should I put a little ad for work in the local weekly and see what comes of it? I have another little job coming up, and quite possibly a whole basement to tape in a few weeks, which is a good start; and I just gave an estimate yesterday for a nice little painting job, so it's not like I'm not trying. I just have to try harder to make sure I've got more work to take some of the pressure off Penny.

In all honesty, Penny would love to move back up north. She has gone up north for her niece's wedding and to visit with her father and sisters and she would love nothing more than to be living up north with her family, and as much as it pained me to tell her the other day over our morning coffee, I did not object to the possibility of us having to sell our house here and moving back up north. I would do it for Penny's sake in an instant, if it every got to that point; but I'm praying it doesn't.

I wish I would have had more smarts going into the game of life, but my parents weren't blessed with that gift. They were too caught up in their own karmic embroilment to learn how the game of life is played and pass their wisdom on to their children. I say this because yesterday I gave an estimate to a Jewish man in Wasaga Beach who wanted some work done on their summer synagogue. Like most people of his race, he was wide-awake to the game of life; but what do I mean by this?

Essentially life is all about survival. We call life a game because there appears to be rules to how life is supposed to be lived; and if we don't know these rules we get chewed up and spit out by life. This is the way it's always been.

I've never had a life mentor, as such. I found my mentors through books, but I've never had a living mentor; so I've had to work my way through the entanglements of life all on my own, and this has cost me dearly—in time, money, and humiliation.

When I met that Jewish man yesterday I could see that he was alive with the knowledge of the game of life. His questions about my estimate for the work to be done on their summer synagogue were quick and to the point, all designed to feel me out and get the best price out of me; but I responded in kind, because I'm experienced enough now to know how the game of life is played. My regret is that I didn't have this knowledge going into life rather than finding it on my way out of life!

Blessed is the child born of parents who pass on the knowledge of the game of life to prepare them for their entry into the working world, because they have a heads up on "old whore life" that will do everything she can to keep one from succeeding. This is just the way it is; but it took me a long time and a lot of heartache to learn this. That's why I'm quick to anger when life throws me a curve like it did this past couple of months.

I'd like to write a story called "Summer Synagogue" to capture this knowledge of the game of life personified by the man I gave the estimate to yesterday. I may get the job, or I may not; but if I do, I'm going to seriously consider writing a story on my experience, because I want to explore this theme of survival wisdom that the Jewish race has wrought out of its inestimably rich experience with "old whore life."

Pardon my metaphor, Padre; but all I mean by "old whore life" is the cruel, vicious side of life that keeps us bound to karma and reincarnation. People know that ugly face of life is like that, but they don't want to own up to it.

We are the "old whore," because we are the authors of our own karmic misfortunes; and learning this is what the journey through life is all about. That's why I wrote my second volume of spiritual musings, *Old Whore Life: Exploring the Shadow Side of Karma.*

As you said, life is all about GROWTH and UNDERSTANDING; but I will explore this in another letter. I remain,

In Spirit,
Your faithful companion,
Orest

20. WHY AM I HERE?

Letters to Ascended Master
St. Padre Pio,
Tuesday, August 30, 2011
6:30 A. M.

Dear Padre,

Yesterday I wrote a spiritual musing and posted it on my blog. It was inspired by something the leader of the New Democratic Party of Canada wrote in his last letter to the Canadian people. He wrote this letter just before he crossed over to the Other Side. He died of cancer after an historic win for his party in the last federal election (2011), which made the NDP (New Democratic Party) the Official Opposition to the governing Conservatives. These were the closing words to his letter:

"My friends, love is better than anger. Hope is better than fear. Optimism is better than despair. So let us be loving, hopeful, and optimistic. And we will change the world."

I called my musing "Love Is Better than Anger," and I wrote it as a tribute to Jack Layton whose funeral and celebration of his life were the best three hours of television that I have ever seen. So moving was the whole service that it went a long way to healing my anger from that last nasty little tempest that blew into my life last month.

God, I was angry! I was so angry from losing my tooth that I wanted to rage at life, and which I did every chance I got. It was the last straw. But watching the service for Jack Layton did me a lot of good. It reminded me of what we are here for.

So, why are we here? Why am I here? That's the more pertinent question. Why am I here, Padre? What's MY PURPOSE in life?

I'm going to share something with you that I'm sure you will appreciate. I've always had the feeling that I made a bet with a group of souls on the Other Side that I could come back into life and find the Way on my own. The bet was that it was impossible to do it on one's own. One has to have a guide to find the Way. I said I could do it on my own, and I was born into my current life and became a seeker at an early age.

I found the Way. I became one of the thirty birds in the Sufi allegory *The Conference of the Birds* that went in search of God and found God and looked into the Face of God. The birds in this allegory had a guide, the hoopoe bird; but I didn't have one, as such.

I found my mentor Gurdjieff at university in Ouspensky's book *In Search of the Miraculous*, which was "miraculously" given to me by a fellow student who thought I should have it, and I followed up on Gurdjieff's teaching of "work on oneself" which got me hooked on a path that linked me up with the "water of everlasting life" that awakened me to the Way; but I did not have a physical guide to show me the Way. I fulfilled my promise of finding the Way on my own, and now here I am writing about it.

So, is this why I'm here; to write about my journey of self-discovery? Is this my purpose in life? You did tell me that you and I had agreed on the Other Side to work together in my current lifetime, which we did with my spiritual healing sessions that became my novel *Healing with Padre Pio,* so obviously you knew that I would find the Way; but here's the rub, Padre—I'm getting tired of writing about the Way!

No; that's not entirely correct. I'm not getting tired of writing about my journey of self-discovery (which is a never-ending process, because I continue to grow in spiritual self-realization consciousness even as I write you these letters); I'm getting tired of waiting for one of my books to connect with the public! It's a fatiguing wait, Padre; and Penny and I are tired of the whole process. *We are very tired!*

But as I said to her last night, "There's nothing we can do about it. All I can do is keep butting my head against the wall." This reminded me of the poem *Invictus*, by William Henley, and I added, "My head is bloody, but unbowed." We just have to keep plugging along the best we can, don't we?

I thought for sure that my blog post yesterday ("Love Is Better than Anger") would attract a few viewers after announcing it on Facebook, Twitter, and Spiritual Networks; but it only brought in fourteen viewers for the whole day yesterday. That's pitiful! I would have thought that there were more people out there who would have loved to read a tribute to Jack Layton, given the incredible service they had for him at Roy Thompson Hall in Toronto on Saturday; but no, only fourteen viewers. How disheartening!

Can you appreciate why Penny and I are tired of the whole process of trying to connect my writing with the public? You did tell me not to worry about finding readers because it was your job and God's job to bring readers to my books; but where are they? Penny and I will be old and crippled before that happens, and what good will that do us?

It may be good for the reader down the road, but it would be so damn nice to see some of the fruits of my years of commitment to writing before it's too late. I've spent a lot of time and energy writing that could have very well gone into making a comfortable life for Penny and myself; so, what's the holdup Padre? What's the point of it all?

I said to Penny yesterday as we talked on the front deck after dinner, "I'm in the land of puzzlement. I can't make heads or tails of it. I thought for sure that my tribute to Jack Layton would break the ice, but it hasn't done a damn thing. I'm stymied."

"So am I," Penny said. How about you, Padre? From over there you can see what's going on down here; so what is going on with my life?

Back to the question: why am I here? But where else could I be? I had karma that had to be worked off here, so I came to work it off. I had a karmic obligation from one of my past lives to be here; so I'm here because this is where I had to be to continue my journey home to God. In fact, we are all here to grow and evolve in our true self; but now what?

I found my true self, and I am growing in my true self; but I am not happy in this part of my journey and I want to know why. Not that I'm unhappy. That's not the case. If you can appreciate it, I'm happy to be where I am in my journey of the self, but I'm unhappy in that I have not yet realized my dreams of connecting with the reading public.

This really bothers me, because in my heart I know that there are millions of readers out there who are just waiting to connect with what I have to share with them, and there's really nothing more that Penny and I can do about it but continue with the process and hope for the best. After all, hope is better than the fear of failure, isn't it?

That's what Jack Layton said in his letter. "Hope is better than fear." Well, Padre; you were called the man of hope and prayer; what do you have to say about my situation? Just keep writing and hope for the best? Is that the answer? Can't this process be sped up; or am I on God's time?

I remain,
Your disconsolate companion,
Orest

21. THE FORBIDDEN KNOWLEDGE

Letters to Ascended Master
St. Padre Pio,
Tuesday, September 6, 2011
6:35 A. M.

Dear Padre,

You told me in one of my sessions that it was to my nature to work out the mysteries of life through my daily experiences, reading, writing, and conversations; well, the other day I finished writing the title musing of my book *Old Whore Life: Exploring the Shadow Side of Karma* and I solved one of the mysteries that has bothered me ever since Gurdjieff introduced me to the concept that nature will only evolve us so far, and to realize our full potential as human beings we have to take evolution into our own hands. The question that haunted me was this: why can't nature evolve us to our full potential?

The answer that came through in my spiritual musing was that the laws of karma and reincarnation govern nature, and to realize our full potential we have to break the cycle of life and death; meaning, we have to break the hold that the spiritual laws of karma and reincarnation have upon us, which can only be done by living the Way consciously.

You lived the Way consciously, Padre. Through prayer and suffering you broke the back of that karmic beast that kept you bound to the eternal cycle of life and death, and you transcended your earthly life; that's why you're an

Ascended Spiritual Master now. But just what does it mean to live the Way consciously?

Few people realize that life is the Way. The mere act of living our life means that we are living the Way, and by Way I mean that we are growing in spiritual consciousness through the karma that we create and resolve with every experience that we have; but we are not conscious of the fact that we are living the Way.

People are not aware that they create karma with every thought, word, and deed; and if the karma they create keeps one bound to the cycle of life and death, one will never realize his full potential, which is to become spiritually self-realized. To realize our full potential we have to live the Way consciously; which means that we have to become aware of the karma that we create. We have to know the difference between karma that keeps us bound to the cycle of life and death, and karma that wakes us up to our spiritual self and liberates us from the cycle of life and death.

At the risk of saying something that cannot be proven, I have a feeling that this knowledge of karma is the forbidden fruit of the tree of knowledge of good and evil that Adam and Eve were told not to eat, because the karma that we create is responsible for the good and evil that we do; meaning, karma that keeps us bound to the recurring cycle of life and death would fall into the category of evil, and karma that liberates us from the cycle of life and death would fall into the category of good.

In effect then, negative karma keeps us bound to life and death; and positive karma liberates us from the cycle of life and death. Religion would call negative karma "sin" and positive karma "virtue," but we must WAKE up to the laws of karma and reincarnation or we will never know whether we are living the Way consciously or not; and that is man's dilemma. So, how do we WAKE up to karma?

Before I answer this, let me ask you: is the knowledge of karma and reincarnation the forbidden knowledge of good and evil? If so, why would God not want Adam and Eve to know this knowledge? Does God want Adam and Eve to grow and evolve in spiritual ignorance? If this is the case, then the serpent's role in tempting Adam and Eve to eat the forbidden fruit of the tree of knowledge does Adam and Eve a service, because it gives them the knowledge on how to live their life and break the endless cycle of life and death. This is a whole new perspective on the serpent, isn't it?

You know Padre, I've been doing a lot of pondering since I had my spiritual healing sessions with you, and I'm beginning to see what you meant when you told me that I have a whole different way of thinking about life; but my perspective is so far outside the box of conventional thought that I feel rather alone out here. Thank goodness you understand me or I'd be really alone!

So, how do I reach the seeker who is ready to step outside the box of conventional thought and find the Way? That's the irony, isn't it—because to find the Way you have to live the Way, and to live the Way you have to step out of the box? How in the hell did I manage to do that? Is this why I saw the image of the "squared circle" in my second year of university when the blue circle of light appeared to me that was then "squared" by a yellow light? Was that a foretelling of doing the impossible—because I did find the Way which liberated me from the paradigm of conventional thought?

It's been some journey, Padre. Just as *la via di sofferenza* was your entry into the Way, mine was the impossible task of "squaring" the circle and resolving the great paradox of life—the paradox of being and non-being!

Anyway, the point I want to make is that mankind is still afraid to eat the forbidden fruit of the tree of the knowledge of good and evil, because to do so would make one conscious of the spiritual laws of karma and reincarnation; and people don't want to assume responsibility for their own salvation—i. e., liberation from the eternal cycle of life and death; hence, mankind's dependence upon the savior principle.

Jesus is the savior principle of the world, but the world doesn't realize that his teaching is all about taking responsibility for our own salvation; but that's an old song, and I really am tired of singing it. This is why I began my novel *Jesus Wears Dockers, The Gospel Conspiracy Story* with the chapter called "Let the World Find Its Own Way," because the world is going to do what it wants anyway. Am I being too cynical?

I really don't think so, because not until a person is ready to eat of the forbidden fruit will they wake up to life. People don't want to wake up to life. This is why life has to wake them up with their own karma! It is ironic, isn't it? No wonder you told me that life is like a joke and we wouldn't get the punch line until we got to the other side!

I remain,
Your amused companion,
Orest

P.S. It just occurred to me that Adam and Eve lived in the Garden of Eden, two souls living in the glorious splendor of earthly paradise; but this perfect splendor did not give them any incentive to grow and evolve into their full spiritual potential. This is why God had the serpent tempt them to eat of the forbidden fruit of good and evil. Good and evil are the two forces in life that promote spiritual growth, because these two forces are always in conflict with each other. Good and evil are the positive and negative karma that we create with every thought, word, and deed; and as we grind and bump into ourselves with the good and evil that we do, we grow in spiritual consciousness until finally, after many lifetimes, we come to the realization that we are spiritual beings trapped in our physical body—just as Socrates said in Plato's *Phaedo*: "There is a doctrine uttered in secret that man is a prisoner who has no right to open the door of his prison and run away." And with this realization comes the desire to escape; and the search for the Way begins!

22. THE MYSTERY OF MY SPIRITUAL HEALING

Letters to Ascended Master
St. Padre Pio,
Tuesday, September 13, 2011
6:30 A. M.

Dear Padre,

It feels like a long time since I wrote you, but I've been spending my creative energies on my spiritual musings. I do miss the closeness that I get with you when I write you a letter, so I'm going to prattle on until the spirit of this letter finds its way.

I've only got thirteen more spiritual musings to write for *Old Whore Life: Exploring the Shadow Side of Karma* and then I can move on to my third edition of spiritual musings; and in all honesty I can't wait to start this new series because I will be tapping into a different level of consciousness—the happy spiritual warrior consciousness.

I wrote a book of spiritual musings on "old whore life" because I wanted to reveal that side of life that we all don't want to face—our shadow self; but it seems that the more light I shed on the Archetypal Shadow (the "old whore" in all of us) the more I incurred the wrath of Satan, who is the collective consciousness of "old whore life." That's why I can't wait to write about the happy warrior, because I will tap into the inherently self-transcending spiritual side of life—i. e., the warrior consciousness of the Way.

Padre, the thought has just come to me that I may be too esoteric for my readers. This thought has come to me many times, I confess; but I resist trying to simplify what can't be simplified—the consciousness of spiritual self-realization.

I've been reading spiritual literature my whole life, and I've never read any book that conceptualizes the Way as I do, which is why I don't want to simplify my writing. I write as the thoughts come to me. I am a servant of my Muse, and I have to trust that my Muse knows what's best for my reader. What do you think?

I realize that most people live by a simple faith, but on the whole this is a blind faith; and all I want to do is shed some light on the human condition. I'd like to share my spiritual insights on life. I realize that life is a journey of the self, but do we have to walk this journey in spiritual darkness? I don't think so. I think the time has come to walk this journey in the light of spiritual clarity; that's why I write as I do—forever seeking to conceptualize the deep mysteries of the Way, or River of God as you call it.

I've been doing some deep pondering on life lately, especially my own life, and just yesterday I felt that I had come to a deep realization about myself. I felt that I was never myself growing up; that I was never real, always phony in some way. This feeling of being false colored my whole life—even after I found the Way and began to live the authentic life of conscious spiritual self-realization; and even after I found my true self!

As much as I didn't want to admit it, I even felt that a part of me was still false after I found my true self, and it wasn't until I met you through my spiritual sensitive and experienced your sanctifying grace did I finally feel totally my true self. It was like your healing energy fit me into myself and I felt something click and I was made whole, and I cannot thank you enough for this spiritual healing.

This is what the journey of the self is all about, isn't it—seeking wholeness. We are forever seeking to be made whole; but what does this mean?

Speaking from my own experience of being made whole through the grace of God (because that's what my spiritual healing was—a gift of God's grace), I can express it this way: being made whole is being true through and through.

This sounds very abstruse, but it's not really. Being true through and through simply means that one is honest in his thoughts, words, and deeds. One does not have a private agenda, as such. One is himself inwardly and outwardly.

Perhaps I can explain this with an image. Imagine an odd shaped block of wood, like a child's building blocks. Imagine another piece of wood with a hole cut into it that is the exact shape as the odd piece of wood. Now imagine trying to fit this odd piece of wood into the hole. It won't fit until the odd shape of the wood matches up perfectly with the hole. When it matches up it will slip into place and the hole will be perfectly filled and the two pieces of wood become one piece of wood. They are made whole, as it were.

That's what I felt like when you healed me, Padre. I felt like I finally slipped into myself and clicked perfectly into place and was made whole! And what a relief it was! For the first time in my life I felt true through and through!

That's why I decided to take on a book of spiritual musings on "old whore life." Being whole, the "old whore" no longer had that subtle hold upon me that she had before my spiritual healing, and I was free to explore her every wile and guile; but it hasn't gone over very well with my readers. They're afraid to read my musings on "old whore life" because they don't want to see their own falseness; and so, life goes on.

Maybe I should clarify what I mean by "old whore life." It may help my reader to understand that "old whore life" is a literary image that I have created to give expression to the natural process of karmic reconciliation. I have created an image in "old whore life" of the psychological, philosophical, and spiritual perspective on how the negative forces of life work in the Divine Plan of God to bring soul into agreement with itself—or, as I expressed it earlier, to be made whole.

In effect, "old whore life"—that nasty side of life that forever seeks to frustrate us at every turn—is in reality doing what she does for our own spiritual good, because she makes us more aware of ourselves; and the more aware we are of ourselves the more responsible we have to be, because with consciousness comes spiritual responsibility.

That's why my readers are afraid to read my spiritual musings—because my musings wake them up to their inherent responsibility to be made whole.

Is this a presumption, Padre? Am I standing on my own pulpit preaching the Word according to Orest? Oh God, I hope not! Please tell me no. I don't want to invite that "old whore" back into my life. I've been down the road of spiritual vanity, and I won't be able to suffer through another tempest of foul winds so soon after my cherry pit fiasco!

If what I have written sounds like I'm preaching, please pardon my presumption; it wasn't meant to be that way at all. All I want to do is share my insights and let the world find its own way to wholeness!

I remain,
Your spiritual companion,
Orest

23. ONE LITTLE EMBRACE AT A TIME

Letters to Ascended Master
St. Padre Pio,
Sunday, September 18, 2011
6: 55 A. M.

Dear Padre,

I'm in a quandary, so I'm just going to pour my heart out and see where it takes me. I know you don't mind listening to me. This is one way that you serve the world, isn't it? Being one with Divine Spirit you are one with the Word, which is the Way and omniscient guiding force of life, or what can simply be called the Voice of God—but that's getting way too esoteric; so let's just keep it simple.

That's my problem, isn't it? I can't keep it simple. I have to dig deeper and deeper and deeper. I'm like a spiritual mole. I have to mole my way into truth, and I never stop digging, and digging, and digging. Well Padre, I'm tired of digging!

Does that mean that I'm tired of myself? I don't know; but I know that life has fatigued me. I had hoped that by this time in my life I would have realized the dream of my literary ambitions, but it hasn't happened yet. I'm published, and I'm proud to have a record of my spiritual journey through life with my novel *Keeper of the Flame*; but I feel that my life is unfinished; and it will not be finished until I tell the whole story.

But what is the whole story? You told me in one of our sessions that even though you are now in that place of all knowing and seeing you were still growing and that you appreciated being of service to me because it helped you to grow spiritually. That took me by surprise. But the more I thought about it, the more sense it made because there is no end to spiritual perfection, is there? God is infinite in its perfection, and the more one serves God the more he grows in the consciousness of God; isn't that so, Padre?

Yes, I hear you say; *God will never stop becoming God. This is the greatest mystery of them all; and the more you embrace it the more sense it makes.*

Embrace what? The mystery of God? The concept of serving God to grow in the consciousness of God? Which?

Both. In serving God, you become more conscious of God; that's the final goal of life. And to serve life you have to embrace life. That's the answer to your quandary. Don't be afraid to embrace life at your age. There is no age to embrace life. It doesn't have to be in a big way. One little embrace at a time. Watering the flowers is a little embrace. Petting your cat and hugging your spouse. Embracing life with love is the key to the art of embracing life. Learn to love what you do and do what you love; that's the sum of all spiritual paths that will take you to the Heart of God and happiness.

And what about life fatigue? Can I overcome my life fatigue with one little embrace at a time? Is that my cure to this debilitating spiritual malaise? I hear you laughing. Did I say something funny?

You sound like a broken record, but I do understand. I too suffered from life fatigue, as you call it. Actually, that's a very good term for spiritual malaise. I won't lie to you. It will take more than one little embrace to cure you of your life fatigue. In truth, it cannot be cured because it is not meant to be cured. It is that state of consciousness that all souls will come to when they are ready to leave this world. You have lived many lives, and you want to come home. That's why you are tired of life. That's your spiritual malaise. I too longed to leave my life. I too longed to go home. Now I'm home and you're still there, but you have more life to live and more books to write. Try not to worry about tomorrow. Let me and God do the worrying for you. Just do what you have been called to do.

I'd love to believe you, Padre; but how can I be sure that this came from you?

What difference does it make? As long as it solves your quandary, does it matter if it came from your own creative consciousness or me?

Not really. But I have my suspicions about "automatic writing." It scares me, because it gives the mind free reign, and that's not a healthy way to go.

True. If it makes you uncomfortable, stop. Just work your way through as you always do, by letting the moving finger write with inspired thought.

One way or the other, I thank you for the insight into my quandary. The answer seems to be the same as always, but it's refreshing to hear it expressed the way it came through this morning—*one little embrace at a time.* I like that!

That's all for today. I have to collect my energies and see if I can embrace my contract work with the same love that I have for writing. Thank you, Padre.

I remain,
Your spiritual companion,
Orest

103

24. THE STATUS OF EGO

Letters to Ascended Master
St. Padre Pio,
Monday, September 19, 2011
8:45 A. M.

Dear Padre,

During one of my spiritual healing sessions I brought up the subject of the selfless self, because I wanted to open the door on the transformative process of the Way. You lived *la via di sofferenza,* which is Christ's way of suffering; and I lived the gnostic path of spiritual self-realization consciousness. Both paths are separate streams of the River of God, and as we lived the Way we had to come to terms with what I called my shadow and you called your "demons." In effect, we had to transform our human self-consciousness with our separate paths; and by this I mean our ego.

Of course, you succeeded much more valiantly; which is why you have come to be known as the Saint of Humility. And, thanks to the devastating power of your humility you slew my vanity and granted me the spiritual healing that I sought. And now I am free to write with much more spiritual clarity on the elusive nature of ego, which is the chief obstacle to man's spiritual salvation.

But I did mention in my session how absurd it would be to try to live Christ's teaching of self-sacrifice in today's consumer world of endless desires. The world simply won't make that kind of sacrifice, and you agreed; which is why we came to the conclusion that the wisest thing to do is to try to bring ego into balance with soul, because Christ's concept of "dying" to one's life to "save" one's life simply won't cut it today.

Padre, you have no idea how happy I was that we saw eye to eye on just how difficult it is to live Christ's teaching of salvation in today's world. In fact, it's almost impossible to live in any world; but that's how Jesus introduced the Way to the world.

I don't know why he had to go to such extremes. Maybe those were extreme times that needed an extreme teaching of the Way, I don't know; but I do know that regardless of how extreme Christ's teaching of self-sacrifice was, he did reveal the essential principles of the Way that can be lived anytime, anywhere. One simply does not have to take them to the extreme that Jesus asked of his times, that's all.

Padre, I can hear my Roman Catholic reader asking if my understanding of Christ's teaching isn't a violation of the truth according to Jesus. After all, he did say, ***"I am the way, the truth, and the life; no man cometh unto the Father but by me,"*** didn't he?

I don't doubt the truth according to Jesus. In fact I love the truth according to Jesus, especially in the book that you recommended for me to read—*Love Without End, Jesus Speaks,* by Glenda Green, the artist who painted the famous portrait of Jesus called "The Lamb and the Lion." But believing the truth according to Jesus on faith alone is vastly different from believing in it with gnostic awareness; meaning, I found the "interpretation" of the sayings of Jesus and experienced my immortal spiritual self.

"Whoever finds the interpretation of these sayings will not taste death," said Jesus, in the *Gospel of Thomas*; and at the risk of offending some readers, few people have broken the code of Christ's sayings. This is why we had a meeting of minds, and why you said to me that you also had found the Way—implying that you understood exactly where I was coming from, which endeared you all the more to me.

So, where am I going with this? Bringing ego into balance with soul, our spiritual self; that's the gist of this letter, which was inspired by something that Lord Conrad Black said in an interview that I saw on TV's W5 the other day.

Conrad Black, a brilliant and dauntingly articulate man with an ego so massive it fills a room the moment he walks in, was a newspaper baron who skillfully managed the takeover of Britain's *Daily Telegraph* that automatically entitled him to a seat in the British House of Lords, and the author of three biographies (Quebec premier Masurice Duplessis, President Nixon, and Presidents Roosevelt) and two memoirs, *A Life in Progress* and his recently published *A Matter of Principle*; but over time Lord Black's fortunes began to reverse, and he was charged with fraud in the United States.

Throughout his very public defense, which he fought valiantly, his wife Barbara Amiel stood by his side; and as painful as it was for Lord Black to suffer the humiliating indignities of public ridicule his head was "bloody but unbowed."

When asked by the interviewer on W5 what he thought of his wife's support during his defense and incarceration in a Florida jail, Lord Black replied that his marriage was too strong to be shaken by the storm of his public humiliation. "I love my wife," he confessed; but then he said something that revealed the incredible hold that his ego still had on him even after all his public humiliation. "But more important, I love the status of being in love with her," he said.

The image of being in love with Barbara Amiel, who is still a strikingly beautiful woman in the autumn of her life, was more important to him than the reality, and I could not help but smile at how he could be so foolish to admit that on camera; but the more I thought about it the more I realized that image characterizes ego, and Lord Black's ego craved to be seen in the public's perception of his enviable position of being in love with his wife.

Ego lives to satisfy all of its desires, and social status is one of ego's most voracious desires; that's why Lord Black said that he loved the status of being in love with his beautiful wife, a successful journalist and intellectual equal, more than he loved her. "She is the epitome of my most ardent desires," he said, when he first fell in love with her; but the image of being in love with her was more important to his ego.

You see Padre, how hard it is to break the hold ego has upon soul? Of course you know this; but I just wanted to make the point that the bigger the ego the more difficult it is to break its hold upon our true self. *What an immovable force ego can be!*

In truth I have enormous respect and admiration for Lord Conrad Black, despite his brutally wounded Ozymandian ego. The vicious forces of "old whore life" came at him with a lustful vengeance, and he's fighting a valiant fight to reclaim his honor.

From all the reviews that I've read so far of his new memoir *A Matter of Principle*, he's fighting the good fight; and I have a feeling that in the fullness of time he will vindicate himself and reclaim his good name. I hope so. That's all for now,

I remain,
Your faithful companion,
Orest

25. EDITING HEALING WITH PADRE PIO

Letters to Ascended Master
St. Padre Pio,
Thursday, September 22, 2011
6: 35 A. M.

Dear Padre,

I've started working on the first edit of *Healing with Padre Pio,* which I began two days ago, and I'm on Chapter 23, "Getting Spiritual Clarity," which is the sixth transcript of my sessions with you, and I'm thoroughly enjoying it because I'm far enough removed from my novel now to read it with fresh eyes—and I love the way you come across!

God, it must be nice being on the Other Side! That's the feeling I got as I read your answers to my cheeky questions. But I had to know. I had an incredible opportunity to exploit your spiritual knowledge as my gifted sensitive channeled you, and I took liberties; but you were so gentle with me that I feel both proud and ashamed of my behavior. Proud because I had the temerity to confront you with questions that put you on the spot, and ashamed that I did; but you understood and answered most of them.

True, you would not commit yourself to some rather embarrassing questions; but your answers were implied in your commentary, which I had to figure out, and this makes for a wonderful read because it adds dramatic tension to my story—like the question I asked about Christianity's belief in one life only, which you knew only too well now from your place of all knowing and all seeing was untrue because soul lives as many lifetimes as necessary to realize its divine nature, and the most you would admit to was that the River of God has many tributaries.

But that's okay. I loved your analogy, and I exploited it to convey the unfolding theme of *Healing with Padre Pio*—i.e., the way of Christian faith and the way of gnosis, which God brought us together to bridge. But how will Christian readers receive this perspective, especially Roman Catholics who obdurately believe that they have proprietary rights to the truth about salvation in their savior Jesus Christ?

You did say that my novel would be controversial, and I have no doubt it will be; but you also said that controversy was good because it generates dialogue, and the world could use a real good honest dialogue on the River of God!

That's the crux of the problem, isn't it—mankind's fixation with its many paths when in reality they are all tributaries of the one River of God?

But the world will always be this way, you said; and regardless which path one is on, it's all about growing in UNDERSTANDING. And when one has grown enough he will see that the River of God flows through all paths in life and that every soul is its own divine tributary—which you called a journey of the self. That's why I'm writing these letters, to give the reader a heads up. But am I being presumptuous?

I hope not, Padre. I don't want to be accused of having contracted the "messiah virus." I've seen what that can do to a person's life. NO THANK YOU! I have no desire to save the world, because the world has its own agenda and does not need to be saved. The most we can do is try to make it a better place than when we came into it; and my little contribution will be the wisdom that I have garnered in my own spiritual quest.

I have always had the good fortune to be guided by books in my search for my true self. In fact, how many times did Divine Spirit drop books into my lap, as it were, as I was working on *Healing with Padre Pio*? At least half a dozen times. So books are a way for a lost soul to find its way home to God, and I hope that my novel *Healing with Padre Pio* will be one of those books!

I remain,
Your faithful companion,
Orest

26. WRITING FROM THE HEART

Letters to Ascended Master
St. Padre Pio,
Saturday, September 24, 2011
8: 45 A. M.

Dear Padre,

While Penny and I were having our morning coffee earlier this morning we got onto the subject of the novel that she's writing, and I made the comment that her writing voice is so much more expressive and evocative than her personality voice, and then I said, "Wouldn't it be something if we could make our writing voice our personality voice?"

"You can't hold on to that voice, though," Penny said. "It would be too much for people, don't you think?"

"Yes and no," I said, which reminded me of my talks with the water color artist who inspired my character Kevin Archer in my novel *The Waking Dream.* His need to find his own way in art was so great that he engaged me on such a deep level that I tapped into Soul consciousness, and he got all the answers that he was looking for; and this, Padre, is what I think you meant when you told me in one of my sessions that I would be writing more from the heart now and not from "out there," which you called "fantasy."

I didn't take offense when you told me that because you had already slain my vanity with the devastating power of your humility, but when I transcribed the tape of my session I felt the full impact of your comment, and in all honesty you forced me to rethink my writing. This is why I've decided to write stories that I have been putting off for years because I did not want to revisit those emotions.

They were too painful, and experiencing them once was enough; but the sad truth is that these stories make the best literature. This is why this morning I was nudged to read some Russian literature—like Tolstoy, Chekhov, and Dostoevsky. In fact I picked up Volume 3 of *Gateway to the Great Books, Imaginative Literature* when I went to the washroom later and selected Tolstoy to read, and I'm going to reread his novella "The Death of Ivan Ilyitch" which is considered to be a work of literary genius.

I want to reread this story to get into that place where I can write from emotional experience, which you call writing from the heart, because I've come to the conclusion that writing from the heart is the best way to connect with my reader. Besides, Penny has always said that my best writing is my story writing. But you confirmed it with your comment about writing from the heart, because the heart is where the truth lies.

Which reminds me of the books that I was inspired to read for one of my sessions with you, books on Jesus; and I have to tell you Padre, the books that I found the most boring were those that came from what you called "out there," because they were pure fantasy—Deepak Chopra's book on Jesus, and Ann Rice's book on Jesus; the more I read these books, the less they held my interest because they lacked gravitas.

A story has to have the gravitas of truth to engage the reader. That's what I think, anyway; which is why I believe the best literature is always autobiographical. And this is why I have decided to revisit those experiences that I didn't have the courage to write about because they were so damn painful—like my study of that offshoot Christian solar cult teaching that did irreparable damage to my eyes.

I have a few more choice experiences that I have also repressed because they were so unbearably humiliating, and I may explore some of them also for my new collection of short stories; but I have to work up the courage to delve so deep into those emotions, so I may start with lesser emotional experiences.

It's all a process, isn't it Padre? But I do thank you for drawing the distinction for me about writing from the heart and writing from the mind. Writing from the mind connects the writer to the world of the mind, which is ephemeral; but writing from the heart connects one to the life process, or what the poet Adrienne Rich calls "that which is," and the closer one can get to "that which is," the more the reader can identify with the story.

In short Padre, I'm going to try to win my reader over with stories that come from my own life, from my heart and not from my mind as such; and I want to thank you again for drawing this distinction for me. That's all for now…

I remain,
Your faithful companion,
Orest

27. ONCE AGAIN, YOU SURPRISE ME

Letters to Ascended Master
St. Padre Pio,
Wednesday, September 28, 2011
5:05 A. M.

Dear Padre,

Once again, you surprised me. I know that you arranged that little coincidence last Sunday afternoon at the library in Barrie that inspired the last chapter of my novel *Healing with Padre Pio,* and I want to thank you for helping to bring my novel to closure.

You told me in one of my sessions (it may have been the last session, I'm not sure) that I would be ending *Healing with Padre Pio* with a question; well, even though I was conscious of what you told me, I still got the surprise of my life—which reminds me, you also told me that my ending was going to be a surprise!

Good God, Padre; if that isn't proof of your presence in my spiritual healing sessions with my gifted psychic who channeled you, then I don't know what is!

Here's what happened: I went to a spiritual worship service in the library in Barrie last Sunday. After the service I walked down to the coffee shop to read my Sunday paper. A friend from the service joined me later. She's a new member of our spiritual teaching and she likes to talk with me. We've become friends. She's in her early eighties, a widow, and a wonderful woman with love in her heart. She sat beside me at the worship service. And beside her sat another widow, in her sixties, who is also a new member but very slow to embrace some of the spiritual concepts of our path, like karma for example.

After the worship service I walked down to the coffee shop and my octogenarian friend with love in her heart stayed and socialized for a while, and when she joined me for coffee she told me about her conversation with the other new member who sat beside her at the service who asked her questions about karma. She couldn't answer her questions and suggested that she talk with me; and wouldn't you know it, that's exactly what happened.

After coffee with my friend I walked back up to the library where I had parked my car; but before going to my car I went into the library to use the washroom. As I entered the lobby I saw the new member who was asking my friend about karma coming out of the library, and I said hi again and before long we were sitting on a bench in the lobby and she was asking me questions about our teaching—and that little coincidence of bumping into her at the library inspired the last chapter of *Healing with Padre Pio,* which came as a complete surprise to me and which ended my novel with the question, "Why bother?"

I couldn't get over how it all came about. I had been putting off writing the last chapter for almost three months, but I was nudged to start it after my experience with the new member who was doubtful about some aspects of the new spiritual teaching that she was studying. She needed answers to her questions and her sincerity engaged me on that deep level where I connect with what Jesus called the "water of living truth," and she got the answers that she needed to hear; and I translated this experience into my fictional last chapter, using this woman as the model for my character who asks the question "Why bother?" that brought my novel to unbelievably satisfying closure.

When I shared with Penny how I had brought *Healing with Padre Pio* to closure with that question, I felt that you were in the room with us and I swear I could hear you giggling in glee because you were so happy with how I had brought my novel to closure. Penny saw an orb in the room, which I know was you; so here we are, Padre. It's all done, and all I have to do now is edit and tighten it up!

As I was saying, even though I knew that you had told me I would be ending my novel with a question, which made me very conscious as I was approaching the end of my chapter, but as conscious as I was about ending my novel with a question I got the surprise of my life when my fictional character unexpectedly came up with the question "Why bother?" *I couldn't believe how it came about!*

It was weird, Padre—because I made happen what you saw would happen three or four months ago and I was conscious of it happening as I was writing the last chapter but totally unaware of how it was going to happen! *What a strange writing experience!*

It was like the past, present, and future were blended together into the Now—the eternal present! I don't know what to make of it, but I think I'm on the brink of something very big here—like I'm about to enter into a new dimension of reality!

You did tell me that I would be discovering through my own life experiences this reality that you called a karma-free life. You told me that karma is soul's choice and that soul can live a karma free life, and this puzzled me; but I think I'm on the brink of discovering how one can do this. I don't know why, but I feel the last chapter that I wrote to my novel *Healing with Padre Pio* has given me the privilege to step into the mystery of a new dimension of spirituality. Am I correct in this?

Whatever it is, I know that something is happening; and this excites me. So I want to thank you for the little coincidence that inspired my last chapter, and I do confess that it came as a total surprise to me—*just as you said it would!*

I remain,
Your faithful companion,
Orest

28. A CHANGE OF PLANS

Letters to Ascended Master
St. Padre Pio,
Wednesday, October 12, 2011
6: 30 A. M.

Dear Padre,

Penny just sent the final proof of *Just Going with the Flow* to our Internet publisher, so we should be seeing it in print by next month; but instead of working on my novel *The Seeker: Quest for the Lost Soul of God* which we had planned to publish next, I was strongly nudged to publish *Healing with Padre Pio* first. Why the change of plans, though?

Whether you nudged me or not, I don't know; but I feel it's the right way to go, because I think *Healing with Padre Pio* will have a better chance of finding its readers than *The Seeker*. Besides, I plan to start publishing these letters on a new blog next month, which I hope will create enough reader interest to jump-start *Healing with Padre Pio*.

I haven't connected with my readers yet, Padre—despite the fact that you told me you and God would bring the readers to my books! Or am I just being impatient? Is it a question of "divine timing," to use your phrase?

The truth is, Penny and I aren't getting any younger; and if we're to see the fruits of our labor before 'time's winged chariot" draws too near, it better happen soon. We're anxious of running out of savings, because our economic situation could get very tight in the next few years. This is why we want one of my books to connect, because it will raise the profile of the others and hopefully we can realize the "glory" of our efforts.

Oh, I should tell you that I rendered the last chapter of *Healing with Padre Pio* down from 3,700 words to less than 1,500 for a CBC short story contest that I will be submitting it to this weekend. First prize is $6,000, and the story will be published in a magazine and the author interviewed by Sheilagh Rogers on CBC Radio's The Next Chapter. That would be great exposure; so Padre, if it's not too much to ask for your help on this one, I'm not too proud to ask. The four runners-up will receive $1,000 cash prize, and have their stories published on the Canada Writes website; also good exposure.

My story is called "Why Bother?" And even though I had to cut the story by 2,200 words, it reads well; and I hope it wins because it will introduce the reader to the spiritual perspective of karma—the divinely redemptive law of love. So Padre, if you want to help me get the message of the River of God out there, this is one avenue; but then, it's all a question of "divine timing," isn't it?

I honestly don't know when it comes to my writing. I've always felt a resistance to my writing that I can't explain. I thought for sure my novel *Keeper of the Flame* would attract more of a readership than it has, but so far it's barely creeping along—despite the auspicious dream that Penny had about the book, which I shared with you in one of my spiritual healing sessions. What is this resistance, Padre?

I can't explain it. The closest I can come is that I believe the negative forces of life don't want the focused point of spiritual light that my writing offers to be introduced into society because it will cause a paradigm shift in the reader's thinking. Didn't you tell me that my writing offers a whole new thought process, a new way of thinking? Is this the cause for the resistance to my writing—the ego consciousness of life does not want to be put under the spotlight? Because that's what my writing does—especially my book *Old Whore Life, Exploring the Shadow Side of Karma*!

People don't want to think the big thoughts. They don't want to spend time figuring out why we are here; they just want to get on with their life. They have much too much to worry about to think about their spiritual purpose in life. They care, but they don't want to spend any energy trying to figure it out. They don't have the energy to spare. What energy they have left after fighting the day's battles with life they spend on getting what little pleasure they can get out of life. The ego takes care of itself first and it leaves little or no energy left to nourish one's soul; that's why the world is in such a mess, isn't it?

And this is the theme of *Healing with Padre Pio*—to bring ego into balance with life, because the scales have tipped too far on the side of self-interest. We have to develop more interest taking care of our planet, because we have let the Garden of Life go to weed. It's a long road to hoe Padre, but if we each do our little part we can make a difference; and my part is simply to introduce some spiritual clarity to social consciousness.

That's enough of my soap box for today…
I remain,
Your spiritual companion,
Orest

29. THE DRY SPIRITUAL DESERT OF ANGER

Letters to Ascended Master
St. Padre Pio,
Saturday, October 15, 2011
7:05 A. M.

Dear Padre,

There's no denying the fact that my spiritual musings on "old whore life" had an effect on me, a subtle shift in consciousness that reached critical mass and put me into a state of anger that I had trouble understanding, and not until I connected the dots and realized why I was so angry at life did I realize that my musings on "old whore life" were responsible; and I decided it was time to move on and write a new set of spiritual musings that would take me out of the dry spiritual desert of anger.

But why this state of anger? What was it about my spiritual musings on "old whore life" that brought about this state of anger?

"Old whore life" is my metaphor for the cruel side of life, that aspect of karma that we don't want to own up to because we are responsible for the cruelty in life, and as my spiritual musings on "old whore life" connected the dots and made the karmic connection so obvious that the reader could not help but see that they are responsible for the cruelty of life, it induced a state of anger; and this anger state of consciousness came back to me from the readers of my musings, and which finally reached critical mass and I could no longer deny my anger at the world. And then I bit into the cherry pit that cracked my tooth and all hell broke loose. And for a good month I was stuck in the dry spiritual desert of anger.

It's not a nice place to be, Padre. Anger is stark and unforgiving. Anger is a state of consciousness that sees the naked truth about man's behavior. The lies, self-deceptions, and hypocrisy are so obvious from this anger state of consciousness that one wants to shout at the world: WAKE UP! But if you do, as I did, no one will hear you; because no one wants to wake up to their lies and self-deceptions. And this only makes one angrier, as it did me. And I became so spiritually parched in my desert of anger that I had to find my way out; so I decided to write a new set of spiritual musings that would induce a new state of consciousness—one of goodness, love, kindness, and compassion. And I found my inspiration in Wordsworth's poem "Character of the Happy Warrior."

I wrote my first happy warrior musing to begin the process, and I began to focus on shifting my attention from the cruel side of life to the spiritual warrior side of life, the valiant side of man's soul that surmounts the struggles of daily life; and I'm going to keep my eyes peeled and ears open for any insight that might inspire a new musing. This way I can facilitate the shift in consciousness from the spiritually dry angry state of "old whore life" to the spiritually quenching state of the happy warrior.

What do you think, Padre? I have to do something, don't I? I had no idea that I would find myself in the middle of a dry spiritual desert of anger when I began writing my musings on "old whore life," because I thought it would simply be exciting to explore the consciousness of "old whore life." It would make a great book, I thought; but I got a hell of a lot more than I bargained for!

I did get a great book. In fact, a psychic friend and member of a book discussion class that I belong to told me that *Old Whore Life, Exploring the Shadow Side of Karma* is going to be my most powerful book; and I can see that happening. These musings are powerful, because they shine the light on the "old whore" and reveal her for who she is—US!

We are "old whore life." We are responsible for the cruelty of life. We are the authors of our own miseries, and these musings make no bones about it; that's why it's going to be my most powerful book. And thank goodness it's almost finished! I've got nine more musings to write and then I can put it aside to wait its turn for publication, because I have several other books to publish first—*Healing with Padre Pio,* and then *Jesus Wears Dockers* that you encouraged me to get out there.

One question, Padre, if I may: did you ever experience this dry spiritual desert of anger? It's been said that you heard up to five million confessions in your lifetime, which could be a bit of a stretch, but you did hear an overwhelming number; and I'd like to know if listening to the sins of your penitents induced in you a state of anger similar to the one that I have called a dry spiritual state?

You must have written a letter to your Spiritual Director about the effect that all those sins you heard in confession had upon you, did you not? I don't recall any from your book of letters (*Secrets of a Soul, Padre Pio's Letters to his Spiritual Directors*), but I cannot imagine you suffering the burden of consciousness of all those sins alone; you must have shared your thoughts and feelings with your Spiritual Director. I'm going to ask you about this when we do our next project together with the woman who channeled you. I'm just curious, because this dry spiritual state of anger is one of the most fascinating states of consciousness that I have explored yet.

But I can't wait to explore the spiritual warrior state of consciousness with my new book of spiritual musings. This state will quench my soul with the loving goodness of life, and it will be a pleasure to write! That's all for now.

I remain,
Your faithful companion,
Orest

30. PRISONER OF MY OWN VANITY

Letters to Ascended Master
St. Padre Pio,
Saturday, October 22, 2011
8: 10 A. M.

Dear Padre,

Thank you for your support yesterday. I finally went for an eye examination, but you cannot imagine—of course you can! You know everything about me! Anyway, I was terrified of going for my eye examination, which I had been putting off ever since my cataract surgery on both eyes three years ago. And I only went to the ophthalmologist in the first place because I was losing my sight because of cataracts; otherwise I would have put it off, and off, and off because I was a prisoner of my own vanity!

This is a bizarre story, and I don't know if I could ever do it justice; but it has to do with that offshoot Christian solar cult teaching that I studied when I was pathologically driven to nourish my newborn spiritual self! Who would believe this, Padre?

I had such a voracious hunger for spiritual energy that I bought into a solar cult teaching said to have been brought into the world by a "Child Christ"—a so called teaching of Light that allowed one to ingest the Logos said to be imbued with the rays of sun, thereby nourishing the spiritual body through sun-gazing techniques!

There may be some deep esoteric truth to this solar cult teaching, but on the surface it was enough to seduce me into taking it up (at the cost of a great deal of money, I might add, because the books and course were not cheap), and I began to practice the solar techniques that ultimately damaged my eyes and so humiliated me in my efforts to explain what I had done to damage my eyes that my ophthalmologist stormed out of the examining room and refused to take me as a patient!

This experience with the ophthalmologist so traumatized me that I developed a phobia for doctors. Thank God the three solar burns I got from practicing the techniques were stationary and not degenerative as the specialists at the eye clinic in Waterloo told me. That's why it took me years before I went to another ophthalmologist when I began to lose my vision because of cataracts. So, Padre, now you can appreciate my comment when I say that stupidity is not a gift of God; it is entirely man made. I have been guilty of such incredible stupidity that I suffered unbearable anxiety for years.

So after my cataract surgery I was supposed to see an optometrist for glasses, but I kept putting it off, and off, and off because I didn't want to have to explain the solar burns in my retinas again; and then Penny had to go to see the optometrist two weeks ago because something was going on with her eyes and I accompanied her.

I bit the bullet and made an appointment; and yesterday 1 went, and because the doctor found nothing seriously wrong with my eyes (I had all kinds of imagined fears) and wrote up a prescription for reading glasses and transition distance glasses, I came home yesterday so relieved from all the anxiety that I had been carting around for years that I had one of the best night's sleep in my life!

I shared this with Penny this morning, telling her that because I am no longer anxious about my eyes I got a great night's sleep, and she was going to say something but I cut her short—*"Don't you dare say it! You can laugh to yourself at my stupidity, but not out loud!"*

"That's no fun," she responded, her eyes laughing.

"I know," I said; and I had to explain why I refused to see an eye doctor all these years, and the one and only explanation was—"it goes to the core of my vanity," I said.

So there you have it, Padre. I was a prisoner of my own vanity for years, and what an incredible feeling it is to be free of the hold my vanity had upon me! Indeed, your redemptive healing energy is still breaking down my vanity, and I have no doubt it will continue to work on my vanity as long as you are with me!

It is such a relief to be free of the anxiety I had for my eyes that I can't thank you enough. I want to go out and celebrate. You were absolutely right when you told me that life is a journey through vanity to humility, which my experience to the optometrist yesterday proved only too poignantly. How unbelievably stupid vanity can make us!

I remain,
Your grateful companion,
Orest

31. A NEW BEGINNING

Letters to Ascended Master
St. Padre Pio,
Tuesday, October 25, 2011
5:05 A. M.

Dear Padre,

My spiritual healing sessions broke down my vanity and gave me room to grow in my wholeness. You said that this was a new beginning for me. I'm not so sure I like this new beginning, though. *I've never felt so vulnerable in my life!*

What bothers me most these days is that I can almost hear "time's winged chariot drawing near." I have so many books already written just waiting to be published and other books waiting to be written that I fear this may not happen before I pass over—which, by the way, I am looking forward to very much because I have grown tired of this life!

So you see my dilemma? I don't want to leave this life because I have too much to write yet, and I want to leave this life because I'm tired of it; and this feeling of mixed emotions is taking its toll on me.

So, just what is this new beginning that you said I had initiated with my spiritual healing sessions with you? Is it new spiritual growth? That would be obvious, given that I no longer have to push against the walls of my own vanity that kept me a prisoner to my spiritual conceit. But that was only one of my many vanity prisons. I may have escaped from that prison, but only recently did I escape from another—the anxiety I suffered for my eyes. I finally took care of that with my eye examination last week!

And what about the tooth I lost? The thought of biting into that cherry pit that cracked my tooth still sends me into a state of rage. I can't help it, Padre; but I just don't see why it had to come to that. Maybe I don't want to see it, that's why it had to come to that; but it sure sent me into a state of rage, and I'm still not quite over it. It was the straw that broke the camel's back. God Almighty, you were absolutely right when you said that life is a journey through vanity to humility!

I would like to reinvent myself. I would like to get back some of that energy of self-discipline that I used to produce by the pounds! I'm getting tired of my life as it is. I can't do the things I used to do physically because of my heart, which has affected how I feel about everything, and it's beginning to weigh heavily upon me. But must I go on whining like this? Where's my gratitude for what I have?

I'm starting a drywall-taping job today. This will get me out of the house and moving again. I short-changed myself on the price that I gave for this job, and I feel absolutely stupid about it; but I will explain this another time. But why wait?

Sunday I gave Jim, the Portuguese man who built his house on the next street over from ours, and for whom I did the drywall taping on the first floor before I had my bypass operation, and now he has hung the drywall in his basement and I gave him a price to tape it, and as I said I short-changed myself by at least a thousand dollars!

Why I did this, I didn't know until yesterday afternoon when it finally hit me while I was reading

Hemingway's Boat while I was in the washroom, a new biography on my literary mentor Ernest Hemingway, by Paul Hendrickson. I don't know what I read that triggered the answer to my dilemma, but I suddenly realized that I short-changed myself on my estimate out of guilt! I was driven by the guilt of not having done the upstairs of Jim's house to my complete satisfaction to give him a rock-bottom price to do his basement!

Guilt blinded me to the reality of the job, and Jim is going to get a damn good price for the amount of work involved in taping his basement. And I'll tell you Padre, in all honesty I beat myself up over short-changing myself because I could not fathom how I could have been so quick to give a price that should have been more thoughtfully worked out. If only I would have stepped back and reflected, but guilt drove me to cut my price by at least a thousand dollars. So a job that should have been twenty-five to three thousand, Jim got for fifteen hundred and it made me sick to my stomach after I gave him that price; and not until it came to me why I did it did I finally come to peace with myself.

So I'm going to do it and heal myself of my guilt. I'm going to work that job to my satisfaction, and live with the loss. I will attribute my loss to what you called "my glory." In other words, the sacrifice that I am going to make will reward me in heaven! And it will, because I'm not going to do this job with any regrets. I'm going to do it with the conscious awareness that I am expiating myself of the guilt I packed around ever since I did the upstairs of Jim's house. Doing the basement for Jim will be a healing experience, and I am looking forward to it because I am tired of repressed guilt, and anxiety, and vanity, and all that bullshit that goes with being so goddamn stupid about life!

Sorry about that, Padre; but it seems that this new beginning is really nothing more than cleaning up my life of all that baggage that's keeping me from living my life the way I so would love to live it—anxiety free, happy, and productive!

That's enough for today!

I remain,
Your faithful companion,
Orest

32. INTIMATIONS OF THE ETERNAL PRESENT

Letters to Ascended Master
St. Padre Pio,
Sunday, October 30, 2011
6: 30 A. M.

Dear Padre,

Yesterday Penny designed the cover for *Healing with Padre Pio*, using a royalty free picture of the archways at the entrance of The Padre Pio Foundation. The archways symbolize the many pathways that lead to the spiritual wisdom of the Way that you reflect in my novel; and the color of the cover is somber, like the robe you wore, and it looks clean and neat—which in a symbolic way reflects my journey of spiritual healing with you in my novel *Healing with Padre Pio.*

To use your metaphor of the river of my life, it was a journey through the muddy waters of my vanity to the clean, clear waters of humility; and what a journey it was. And I'm still riding the currents to even cleaner waters of humility!

But I don't want to dwell on that now. I've gone through my dry spiritual desert of anger and through the dense fog of my unbelievable stupidity, and only now am I beginning to feel some peace of mind from the stark confrontation with the unresolved nature of my karmic self, and I'd like to rest a while before I ride down those currents again; so, if I may, let me move on to something else.

I'd like to know if the ripple effect that you talked about in one of my sessions is beginning to happen, because I've been getting readers from all over the world visiting my spiritual musings blog. You said it would take three years, and then the ripple effect would bring some return to my writing, and I was wondering if this has begun to happen; or was it three years after *Healing with Padre Pio* gets published?

Speaking of my blog, the first edition of my musings has been released. It's called *Just Going With The Flow, And Other Spiritual Musings*. I hope this book attracts its readers. You told me not to worry about it because you and God would bring readers to my books, and I can't wait for this to happen because I'd like to see some action soon—especially for Penny's sake. She puts everything she has into getting my books out there, and I'd like to see it happen before time's winged chariot catches up to us.

Padre, I have a thought skirting about at the edge of my mind that wants to come forth, but for some reason it is hesitant to do so. I can't quite conceptualize the thought, but it has to do with my general feeling about life; a new feeling, one that seems to be a transformation of everything that I have lived by and believed in. It seems to be a whole new thought process, a whole new way of looking at life.

I can't put my finger on it, but I have a strange feeling that I have stepped into a new dimension of reality, a different state of consciousness which allows me to see and experience life in an entirely new way. This is an odd feeling, because old thought patterns won't let go so easily, and there is a kind of reluctance to step forward; but I cannot help the gravitational pull to this other state of consciousness!

I honestly think it's that state of consciousness you said I would be researching where Soul chooses to live karma free. The thought alone freaks me out, because it's so far removed from my paradigm of the cause and effect consciousness of life.

Is this that state of synchronicity where one is always in the Now? Am I getting intimations of the Eternal Present, the Holy Now as Jesus called it in Glenda Green's book *Love without End, Jesus Speaks*?

When I asked you how I would research this state of consciousness where Soul lives a karma free life, you told me I would do so the way I always get my information from life, by squeezing the goodness out of every little experience until I get the essential wisdom of that experience, and also through writing; which you said I would be doing from the heart now. In fact, my spiritual sensitive said that she saw a pen, paper, and a heart; which symbolized my writing life. So, am I going to be writing more from the heart now?

Actually, I have to say that I am; because I feel more deeply these days. I am not blocked by my own vanity as I used to be—or my unbelievable stupidity! As I've already said, vanity makes us stupid; and I had an incredible amount of vanity! But I'm not going there now. I have to give myself a break from that excruciating part of my journey.

I've edited *Healing with Padre Pio* another time since I wrote you last, and I keep getting more out what you revealed to me in my transcripts. It's like what you had to say didn't quite seep all the way in, and with each reading I get a little more; and, to be honest with you Padre, I'm both excited and nervous about how my novel is going to be received because I know it's going to shift some paradigms!

I have to bring firewood into the garage today. The weather is about to catch up to us, and I don't want to do this in the snow. We also have more leaves to rake. We've done leaves three or four times already, but the trees have not all shed yet. The maples have shed, but the oak trees don't shed until late fall, and we have a few oaks in our yard; but we're going to do more leaves today, if the weather permits. Until the next time,

I remain,
Your faithful companion,
Orest

33. THE EGOLESS SELF

Letters to Ascended Master
St. Padre Pio,
Saturday, December 3, 2011
9: 10 A. M.

Dear Padre,

I think I caught a glimpse of how one can live the karma-free life. You told me this was possible, that it was a different state of consciousness; well, yesterday as I was sanding the drywall of the house I'm working at I caught what I believe to be that state of karma-free consciousness, which I recognized as my egoless self.

Yesterday was the fifth day of sanding drywall, and my body was exhausted from the intensely physical work all week. When my body is exhausted like this it frees my mind in a peculiar way. It puts me into a state of awareness, with no thoughts, or judgments, just awareness. Yesterday I tried to hold onto this state of awareness, and the more I held onto it the more I confirmed it to be an egoless state of consciousness.

I felt like I was a self without the burden of my ego. That's why I called it an egoless self, and then it hit me: this is that state of consciousness that you must have meant, because one just *is* in this state. One is Soul, free of ego; and it felt right to think that this was the state of consciousness where one could live his life karma free.

It makes sense. The ego is our human self, which is the self of *being* and *becoming*—our karmic self, if you will; and if we transcend our karma self it follows that we could live a karma-free life. I know this may sound far-fetched, Padre; but I honestly feel I'm onto something with this insight. I think I may have opened the door to the mystery!

This is what I believe we're going to explore in our next book. I don't know when I'm going to initiate this project because I've got my hands full getting *Healing with Padre Pio* ready for publication, and I've also started editing *Jesus Wears Dockers*, so it may be a while yet; perhaps next summer some time. But I will keep notes as the insights come to me on the egoless life, because that's where I think we will be going with our exploration of the wisdom of *Ecclesiastes*, which will be our entry point into our next project.

Padre, a new book on your life has just been published called *Padre Pio: Miracles and Politics in a Secular Age,* by Sergio Luzzatto, and it just won an award for best historical work. I don't know the name of the award, but I looked the book up on Amazon and read the reviews and some really hate the book and some like it. It seems that the controversy over your life and stigmata continues!

I will be ordering the book, as well as the second volume of *Pray, Hope, and Don't Worry, True Stories of Padre Pio,* by Diane Allen that has just been released because I love reading anything about your life, especially about the people that you have helped.

Now, if I may, I'd like to get a bit more personal. I don't really know where I am going with this, but I know that I have to reconnect with my Muse because I feel at a loss when the creative juices are not flowing freely; and they have not been flowing freely since I began taping the drywall of the house that I'm still working on. This house has taken up all of my creative energy, but I am almost finished the job. I have three more days of work and then I can let my creative well fill up again and get back to writing.

Providence pointed to this on Sunday when Penny and I went to Barrie for groceries and we ended up going to Chapters and I bought four magazines and a new book on my literary mentor Ernest Hemingway called *The Hemingway Patrols,* by Terry Mort. The magazines I bought were literary, and I got the strongest feeling that I am to get into story writing from the heart, as you said I would be doing in one of my sessions; that's why I can't wait for my creative well to fill up again because I want to see what my Muse has planned for me. Whatever it is, I have a feeling it's going to be exciting!

Something is going on in my life, Padre. I'm going through a change of life. I don't know what to call it. Perhaps a transformation of consciousness, like I'm in transition from a binary philosophy of life to a more unified, comprehensive philosophy of life in which I take into account all the contradictions of man; and, to be very honest with you, it feels good to see and accept human nature in all of its contradictions!

This is a wonderfully refreshing perspective, because I am not judgmental in this new state of consciousness. I see the faults of man without judging them. What an incredible place to be! It's so liberating! I hope I can grow in this new state of consciousness!

That's all for now…

I remain,
Your faithful companion,
Orest

34. FOR THE SAKE OF TALKING

Letters to Ascended Master
St. Padre Pio,
Sunday, December 4, 2011
7: 05 A. M.

Dear Padre,

I just want to talk with you this morning. I miss my sessions with you. I looked forward to talking with you every month, and I can't wait to begin our next project. I don't have a title for the book yet, but it will come when the time is right. I have the strongest feeling that it will be an exploration of that state of consciousness you referred to as the karma-free life, and I can't wait.

A curious thing happened last night. A woman from Toronto who has a cottage here in Georgian Bay not far from our house called and asked if she could come for a cup of tea because she needed company, so we invited her.

Penny put on a pot of tea and a platter of snacks; cheese, baguette slices, roasted eggplant and red pepper, and butter tarts. Jane (not her real name) stayed for several hours just talking and unwinding, and when she left she thanked us for our hospitality. She did not want to be alone last night, for whatever reason, and when she left she was feeling a lot better. She did not disclose any serious problem, nor did we ask. We just let the evening unfold on its own, and I think she got the healing energy that she needed; so, thank you Padre for being there with us for our friend.

Her visit last night led me to wonder about the new attitude that I have adopted with my friends and acquaintances. I've decided to go into sanctuary. Sanctuary is my refuge from the world. It's the place I used to go to whenever life beat up on me, and life has been beating up on me these past few months, to the point in fact where I could not take it anymore and decided to go to sanctuary; and when I go to sanctuary life begins to change its attitude towards me. That's why I think Jane asked to visit us last night.

Jane's visit was Spirit's way of telling me that life is going to come to me now, that I don't have to make all those efforts that I used to make to meet life on happy terms when all I got back from life was rebuff, resistance, and indifference. I think Jane's visit is a turnaround in my relationship with "old whore life."

And speaking of the "old whore," I've only got seven more spiritual musings to write for *Old Whore Life, Exploring the Shadow Side of Karma*. I'll sure be glad to get this project out of my hair. I never thought I would be stirring the pot as much as I have with this book. It irked the ire of "old whore life," and she came at me with a vengeance; but it will soon be over and I can get on with my third edition of musings.

Penny has started editing *Healing with Padre Pio*, and I'm relieved to see that she actually likes it. I was apprehensive, because she did not warm up to my spiritual healing sessions with you. She likes the story, but feels that some of the transcripts are much too long and would like to see them tightened up. I agree with her, and I look forward to the challenge of tightening them up. And since this is our project, I would like a little help on tightening them up; so, if you would Padre…

Out of curiosity, last night I looked up my sequel to *Jesus Wears Dockers,* my talks with St. Paul, which I called *St. Paul's Conceit* because I wanted to see how this book read. You told me this book has its place out there also, but that it wasn't as well done as *Jesus Wears Dockers;* and I could see that as I read the first chapter. It needs work, but I'm not ready yet to take on the editing. I want to write some fresh stuff first. I have a strong need to let my creative self flow freely in some new stories!

I'm not sure which story I'm going to take on first, but it may be "We May Be Tiny, But We're Not Small," or "La Famiglia," or "The Incident," or "The Cherry Pit." I would very much like to make a book out of these stories and call it *We May Be Tiny But We're Not Small, and Other Stories.* What do you think?

Thanks Padre. That's all for now…

I remain,
Your faithful companion,
Orest

143

35. AN INTERRUPTED LETTER

Letters to Ascended Master
St. Padre Pio,
Saturday, December 31, 2011
7: 15 A. M.

Dear Padre,

It's been a while since my last letter, but I tried once or twice to write you and couldn't connect with my Muse. Something was holding me back.

I've been very busy editing *St. Paul's Conceit*, which I finally finished (I have many more edits yet, but I was called to work on it), and I've also been working on *Healing with Padre Pio*; so I haven't had the creative energy to write you a letter, or write any new spiritual musings for *Old Whore Life*. I've only got seven more musings to write and I'd like to get them done; but I'm just not called to write them yet. I'm waiting for my Muse.

I've been getting some rather curious information lately, which I know is related to my new project with you and which I believe has to do with exploring vanity, because the more I think about it the more convinced I am that life is a journey through vanity to humility. As a matter of fact, just last night as I was drifting off to sleep I got flashbacks of my life, experiences that I saw in a whole new light—*as if through the eyes of vanity!*

Sunday, January 1, 2012
5: 30 A. M.

Sorry, Padre; the power went out yesterday while I was writing my letter and I never got back to it after the power came back on a few hours later. We had freezing rain during the night and I think some hydro wires went down. In any event, Penny and I went out and did some shopping and when we got home I sat in front of the fire and read my paper and new book that I bought, *What the Dog Saw,* by Malcolm Gladwell.

I'm sure this book was brought to my attention by providential design, because it speaks to what I've been thinking about the past week—the moment. This is a book of essays that Malcolm Gladwell wrote for the *New Yorker Magazine* and have been lauded for their anecdotal brilliance—which addresses the literary imperative that I have given myself for my own writing, an imperative that was inspired by you telling me that I am going to be writing more from the heart after my spiritual healing sessions with you.

I'll let you know what I think of the book after I finish reading it, but judging from what I've read so far I think I'm going to not only enjoy this book, but glean a lot of wisdom from this man—both literary wisdom and life wisdom.

To give you an example of literary wisdom, he writes in his Preface: *"Good writing does not succeed or fail on its ability to persuade. It succeeds or fails on the strength of its ability to engage you, to make you think, to give you a glimpse into someone else's head,"* and for an example of life wisdom, he writes: *"People at the top are self-conscious of what they say (and rightly so) because they have position and privilege to protect—and self-consciousness is the enemy of 'interestingness.'"*

Anyway, happy New Year Padre! I know that on the Other Side you are no longer frustrated by the constraints of time and space, but we have to contend with it down here; and I can only hope that this coming year will bring Penny and me the grace and comfort of a successful, happy, and healthy future.

Last night Penny and I were invited for dinner at our neighbor Tony's house. He's the man whom I believe you blessed with your healing grace. Remember my story of how I thought you were "working my neighborhood"? I know you had a hand in bringing the widows Tony and Maria together, and they seem to be doing very well; so, if I may take the privilege on behalf of Tony and Maria, thank you for their companionship.

Today I'm going to put on another fire and finish reading yesterday's paper and get into *What the Dog Saw.* We have a friend from Toronto coming for dinner. She's the woman who called us up one evening to talk. Penny and I listened, but didn't probe. She invited us for dinner last week and revealed something very personal that she wanted to run by us; that's why she wanted to talk that night. So in all likelihood we'll be hearing about the unfolding drama of her personal life today, and I think your healing grace will do her a lot of good; so, Padre, if you would be so kind…

I really don't have much else to say, except that I'm glad to be tapping into my creative consciousness again because I miss the excitement that comes with the thrill of discovery every time I write something new. In fact, this phrase "thrill of discovery" jumped out at me yesterday afternoon when Penny and I were watching TV and I jotted it down on my notepad because I know I'm going to be writing a spiritual musing called "The Thrill of Discovery"—which comes, of course, whenever we tap into the creative energy of the River of God that flows through life.

The River of God is the creative life force, and we tap into it when we connect with our inner self; but I'll get into that when I write my musing. So, *ciao* for now Padre, and I'll be writing you again soon…

I remain,
Your faithful companion,
Orest

36. WHEN ALL IS SAID AND DONE

Letters to Ascended Master
St. Padre Pio,
Saturday, January 14, 2012
8: 10 A. M.

Dear Padre,

I've been hard at work editing *Healing with Padre Pio,* and I'm happy to say that I have cut the manuscript down by fifty pages so far, which really tightens up the story—to Penny's joy. She thought that the transcripts were much too long, and most of my cuts have been made in the transcripts. I may be able to squeeze a few more pages out of them, which will make her even happier; but I have to confess, they do read a lot better. I hope to have my edit finished by the end of next week, and then I can go through the whole manuscript once more before I give it Penny for her next edit.

There was much more work than I expected; but then, I was told by a friend in our spiritual community that this was going to be a big project. She's psychic, and every so often she tells me things about my books that surprise me; and she told me that my book based on my spiritual healing sessions with you was going to be bigger than I thought, and she was right. But I don't mind working on it, because every time I go through it I *hear* a little more of what you had to say to me.

I've been doing a lot of research online lately. I've been exploring C. G. Jung's life and teaching, and given what I've discovered I'm looking forward to reworking my novel *The Waking Dream*. In this novel, Carl Jung came to me in a dream and we talk about one of my books that has been published on the Other Side but not out here yet; but I would like to flesh my Carl Jung character in now that I know more about his life.

Coincidentally enough, a movie on the Jung-Freud relationship has just been released. It's called *A Dangerous Method*, directed by David Cronenberg, and I can't wait to see it. It won't come to Barrie for a while yet, but I'm looking forward to it. Does this coincidence have to do with what you called "divine timing"?

In other words, are Carl Jung's insights into the psyche of man finally ready for mass consumption? Because if so, this means that my novel *The Waking Dream* is being called to be published, because it addresses society's need for a fresh perspective on life.

In any event, I'm excited by the research that I'm doing because it will give me the foundation that I'm going to need for our next project. I just know that all of my research is building a solid foundation for my next book with you, whose theme is going to be about man's journey through vanity to humility, because I'm beginning to see a pattern to the research that I'm inspired to do—and I say "inspired" because I have the uncanny suspicion that you are nudging me from the inner in my research.

Now that I'm a little more proficient on the Internet, I'm exploring more and getting all kinds of interesting information. I've been researching Gurdjieff and his teaching online also, and last night I even watched the move on the net based on Gurdjieff's book *Meetings with Remarkable Men*, plus a documentary film based on

Ouspensky's book *In Search of the Miraculous*, which was about his relationship with Gurdjieff. This brought back all kinds of memories of my time studying Gurdjieff's teaching, and you know what Padre? I'm eternally grateful for having Gurdjieff come to me in that period of my life!

Just as I'm grateful for you coming into my life! I'm becoming more and more appreciative of my relationship with you as I work on *Healing with Padre Pio,* because the more I work on it the more convinced I am of the enormous progress that I have made in my quest for answers to life's meaning and purpose!

I've been doing additional research on Gnosticism online also, and Buddhism, and the deeper I get into the research the more confident I grow in my own writing— because I have connected dots that no one else seems to have connected!

That's why Jung came to me in my dream. He read my book *The Way of Soul* on the Other Side and wanted to ask me some questions about the "alpha and omega of the self," which I have worked into my novel *The Waking Dream*; but I'm convinced now of my contribution to the living Way—and by "living Way" I mean the unfolding consciousness of the Way as it is being revealed to the world by those souls that have tapped into the waters of everlasting life—i. e., the River of God.

I have tapped into the River of God. This is what these letters are all about—giving expression to my spiritual insights as they are revealed to me. Which brings me to the point of this letter: when all is said and done, the Way is right here, in the very experience of one's daily life. One doesn't have to go on a quest like Gurdjieff did to find the answer to the meaning and purpose of life; or delve into the mythologies of the world or ferret out the hermetic secrets of the Gnostics and Alchemists like Jung did. All one has to do is live their life in the conscious knowledge that the River of God runs through all of life, and all one has to do is learn how to tap into the River of God to give his life all the meaning and purpose one could hope for—which is precisely what my writing is all about!

I remain,
Your faithful companion,
Orest

37. I'M LIVING IN A PARALLEL UNIVERSE

Letters to Ascended Master
St. Padre Pio,
Wednesday, January 25 2012
7: 10 A. M.

Dear Padre,

Penny had an appointment yesterday morning at the clinic in Midland to get an x-ray of her right foot which has been bothering her for the last couple of weeks, and a bone density scan as well, and she asked if I would accompany her.

"Of course, sweetheart; you know you're my first priority," I said, in reference to the comment that I made to her one morning a few years ago when she asked if she could have a second morning cup of coffee with me in my writing room, which she knew would cut into my precious writing time, and to my surprise I said to her, *"Sweetheart, I used to have priorities; but now I have you. Of course you can have another cup of coffee with me,"* and that's how we began our morning ritual of coffee together in my writing room.

I dropped Penny off at the clinic and drove across the road to the Zehrs store to pick up some quick rising yeast for the focaccia that I wanted to make for dinner, and I was back in the waiting room before she was done. I don't recall exactly if I told Penny on our drive home from the clinic, or if I had told her over morning coffee, but I shared with her the excited feeling that I got about our next project together.

I did ask you if we would be working on another project, and you said that our work was not yet done; and for the last couple of months I've been online researching, following my nudges—starting with my research on C. G. Jung, then Gnosticism, Alchemy, the Essenes, and onto contemporary spiritually-minded people like Jungian analyst Marion Woodman, Deepak Chopra, Andrew Harvey, and others; and I began to notice a pattern unfolding, all leading to the concept of synchronicity and parallel universes—which all seemed to point to our next project together!

Now I'm in a state of excited anticipation, because I can't wait to get *Healing with Padre Pio* published so we can start our next project. I don't quite know how it's going to unfold, but I have the uncanny feeling that it will have to do with a whole new perspective on karma and evolution. I say this because of the dreams I've been having. I've been dreaming of my hometown a lot more than usual, and I suspect that these dreams have to do with the first time I lived my life in my hometown. You told me that upon completing that lifetime I chose to relive that same life over again, but this time for the purpose of creating a different outcome because the first outcome was unsatisfactory.

It took me completely by surprise when you told me that my life today is the second time around in my same life. But strangely enough, it resonated because I've always had the feeling like I was stuck in my life and had to break free—which I did. And this is why I got to live my same life over again, *so I could create a different outcome!*

You told me that the first time I lived my life as Orest Stocco in the small town of Nipigon, Ontario I was not open to what you called "that other religion" (which is the spiritual path that I am on today), so I was reborn back into my same life so I could create a different outcome and be open to other spiritual paths, which I am today. This is why all of my research recently has created a pattern that seems to be pointing to the concept of synchronicity and parallel universes—because the life I'm living today as Orest Stocco in Georgian Bay, South Central Ontario I'm living in a parallel universe to the life I lived in another universe as Orest Stocco in Nipigon, North Western Ontario. Wow!

This is exciting stuff, Padre! This opens up a whole new perspective on how Soul evolves through life to become aware of the *I Am Principle* of God! I'm so excited that I don't know what to say! In fact, I think I have to sign off now, because this insight has just blown me away—*that I'm living my own life over again in a parallel universe!*

I'm living both of my same lives simultaneously in parallel universes, but in my second lifetime now I have created a different outcome from my first life!

I have to pause….

I remain,
Your faithful companion,
Orest

38. FINDING MY WAY, AGAIN

Letters to Ascended Master
St. Padre Pio,
Sunday, January 29, 2012,
6: 55 A. M.

Dear Padre,

I'm in that place where I feel like I have to find my way again. I'm not lost; I'm just in a strange place, like I've taken a turn around a bend in the river of my life and I don't see any familiar landmarks. I'm not really frightened, but I am a bit disconcerted; that's why I'm writing this letter. I want to see if I can orientate myself.

Although not much seems to have happened in my life since I had my ten spiritual healing sessions with you, everything in my life has changed; but it's hard to explain what I mean by this. It's as though everything has changed, but nothing has changed; a paradoxical state of consciousness that seems to describe the new bend in the river of my life.

I have noticed one obvious difference in my life lately: I tend to cry very easily these days, as though my heart has been pried open and emotion pours out of me whenever I witness an act of kindness, love, compassion, mercy, forgiveness—any act of goodness. I can't help myself. I cannot hold my love in, and it pours out in tears.

I guess this is a good thing. You did tell me that I would be writing more from my heart than from my mind, so I guess this is just a sign that it's starting to happen. But here's my theory about this new bend in the river of my life.

I believe your presence in my life is affecting my consciousness. Ever since we connected in my spiritual healing sessions, your energy is affecting a change in me; and one of the signs of this change is how easily I am touched by any act of love now. It's as though whenever I witness an act of love in people it resonates with something so deep in me that it affects me on an emotional level and my heart is opened and I well up with tears.

As I said in one of our sessions, your love is a redemptive love because you took on the passion of Jesus Christ whose love for man was boundless, and as your energy affects my state of consciousness by your daily presence in my life I am connecting with people in a different way—with compassion. *Eureka!*

When I asked you in one of my spiritual healing sessions to give me a simple definition of redemptive love, you didn't even blink. "Compassion," you said. Has my heart been opened to compassion? Is this why I tear up so easily these days?

Penny and I have watched several very touching movies together this past month, the last one being *Extremely Loud & Incredibly Close,* and I was moved to tears to the point where I said to Penny, "Am I becoming a mush, or what?"

"No," she said; "you're heart has been pried open, that's all."

She can see it, Padre; but it's all very strange, this new bend in the river of my life. Not that I wasn't touched by life before, I certainly was; but now it seems to have magnified a hundred times. And I have to attribute it to my spiritual healing.

Every since your humility devastated my vanity I haven't been the same. I no longer judge people like I used to. I am no longer quick to be right. I see people differently now, from a perspective that understands them more. In fact, I think I've even caught a glimpse of what our next project is going to explore—the multidimensionality of spiritual growth; meaning, karma and parallel universes.

But that's too big an idea to ponder now. I just wanted to orientate myself a little today. Until next time…

I remain,
Your faithful companion,
Orest

39. GOING WITH LIFE AND THE LIVING

Letters to Ascended Master
St. Padre Pio,
Sunday, February 19, 2012
6:35 A. M.

Dear Padre,

It's been almost three weeks since my last letter, but it feels like years; that's how much I feel I have distanced myself from where I was, and I attribute this to all the research that I have been doing online for *The Summoning of Noman.*

I didn't tell you, but I was inspired to start a new book. I wonder if this is the book that you foretold me about in one of my sessions. You said I would be doing research on the karma-free life, and I don't know how it's connected but my new research on C. G. Jung and the individuation process and dreaming has given me an insight into parallel worlds, and I suspect this is connected with the research you said I would be doing on the karma-free life. In any event, I love the research I'm doing.

Jesus said in *Love Without End, Jesus Speaks* to go with life and the living, not the dead and dying, and my research has taken me right into the currents of life and the living with such authors as Caroline Myss (*The Anatomy of the Spirit*), and Gregg Braden (*The Divine Matrix*), to name two writers that have caught my fascination; and what I'm learning about how Divine Spirit is revealing the Way to the modern world is absolutely fascinating. And I know that my novel *Healing with Padre Pio* is going to make an exciting contribution to what can simply be called the living Way.

I'm excited by the new book I started to write. I've got twenty-five pages written, and I'm well into the entry point of my book, with ideas coming all the time on where the book is headed; but I can't get back into it until I finish editing *Healing with Padre Pio.* I have to read it and tighten it up one more time before I give it back to Penny; and then she's going to convert it to a PDF file to begin the process of getting it published.

Padre, your comment about me reliving my life over again to change the outcome, because I wasn't happy with the first outcome of my life has excited my curiosity so much that I think it's becoming the central motif of my new book—which is why I've started keeping a new dream journal.

Dreams are a gateway to the other worlds, and I've been having a lot of dreams of my life in my hometown; but the curious thing is that I feel that many of my dreams have to do with my life the first time I lived it in my hometown, the life that you said whose outcome I wasn't happy with and wanted to change; that's why I came back into my same life to live it over again to change the outcome. So I think my dreams of my life in my hometown are dreams of my parallel life, not my current lifetime; and I find this fascinating!

I don't know where you expect me to go with this, but I'm going to explore this with my new book. I do have a title, by the way; but I won't mention it now. I want to keep this project hush, because I have to preserve the energy of this book, and revealing it before its time would only dissipate the energy of the book.

Anyway, I just wanted to touch base with you again. I miss writing you, and I hope I get back into my habit of letter-writing because it keeps me connected to your energy, and I need your redemptive love energy to keep me humble!

Speaking of keeping me humble, I said something to Penny yesterday morning—or, rather, something came out of my mouth that made her cry. I hurt her with my words, and I felt so stupid for the mindless cruelty of my words that I said to her, "I'd rather stab myself in the heart than hurt you," and I apologized for my insensitive remark.

I said to Penny later that I thought I had pulled my vanity out by the roots with my spiritual healing sessions with you, but given my insensitive remark obviously I hadn't pulled out all the roots; that's why I have to stay connected with your humbling energy. So, indulge me please...

I remain,
Your still-humbling companion,
Orest

40. MY NEW BEGINNING HAS BEGUN

Letters to Ascended Master
St. Padre Pio,
Monday, February 20, 2012
10: 47 A. M.

Dear Padre,

I'm having fun in my new discoveries. Here's a little poem I wrote just a few minutes ago that was inspired by the online video, *David Whyte: Companionship with the Disappearing Light.* The poet is talking about the way of the artist, and the courage it took the artist Jerry Wennstrom to go on his quest, which every seeker must do when he or she has heard the Call of Soul. I call my poem, "They Found Me."

> I found a poet,
> whose way is poetry;
> I found a healer,
> whose way is healing;
> I found a scientist,
> who found the Way;
> and I am happy
> they all found me.

You did tell me in my last or second-last session that this was a new beginning for me; well, I'm beginning to experience this new beginning. It started with my rekindled interest in dreams, which opened the door to many areas of research that is exciting my creative spirit like it hasn't been excited for a long time.

It started with my research on C. G. Jung, which opened up doors to other Jungian analysts and the way of the dream, which opened up doors to Gregg Braden (the scientist in my poem), to Caroline Myss (the healer in my poem), and to David Whyte (the poet in my poem); and the reason I'm so excited by these people is because they have found the Way in their interests and are giving it expression through their own life path.

This excites me, because I'm finally finding people who live the Way in their own life—and not some exclusive teaching like the members of my spiritual community, who to my mind have restricted the Way to the most direct path home to God and thereby miss out on the richness, beauty, and endless joy of the Way in life at large; so thank you, Padre, for my spiritual healing sessions with you, because your humility devastated the vanity of my own spiritual path and brought me back to the Way of my own life.

I drove into Midland yesterday and bought two books by Gregg Braden (*Deep Truth*, and *Fractal Time*), and one book by Caroline Myss (*Entering the Castle*); and I made an appointment for Penny's car at Canadian Tire, which I had a little accident with Saturday morning when I drove her to Barrie to catch the bus for Toronto where she was flying out to Thunder Bay to visit her father who was just put into a nursing home.

I slid into a curb in the fresh snow and knocked the tires out of line and have to get the car fixed before Penny returns. That whole experience was a waking dream, which I am going to write about in my new novel, and which I'm going to couple with another waking dream I had yesterday while watching a Gregg Braden video (*The Language of the Divine Matrix*), so I need not tell you about them here.

As unpleasant as both of my waking dream experiences were, the message they gave me was so revealing about one of my character flaws that I'm ever so grateful for having had those experiences—*whatever they cost me!*

I just thought I'd share this with you, Padre; because I believe this brings me closer to our next project. I just feel that I'm well into my research for our next project, which I honestly think is going to be about how to live the Way the modern way.

Until the next time…

I remain,
Your faithful companion,
Orest

41. THE FINAL EDIT OF MY NOVEL

Letter to Ascended Master
St. Padre Pio,
Friday, March 9, 2012
5:55 A. M.

Dear Padre,

I completed the final edit of *Healing with Padre Pio* yesterday and last night Penny converted it into a PDF file. She got the ISBN number for the book, and now she's going to work on getting the cover ready. We hope to get the book out by next month.

I don't know how many times I read through the manuscript. Maybe thirty times, and I am convinced that I can't do any more for it. I scrolled through the PDF file last night and liked how it read, and I hope the reader does too.

I don't know what to say about this book, Padre. The experience of working with you for a spiritual healing has done wonders for me. You brought me a long way in a short time, and I honestly don't know how to thank you for guiding me on my journey through vanity to humility.

I hope my novel will help my reader realize what's important in their life, because life really is all about this journey through vanity to humility; but then what? Where am I headed now?

Well, life goes on in the same way it went on before, but only now life has a different flavor. Life no longer speaks to me the way it used to. I no longer see life the way I used to. Life is the same, but because I've rid myself of the vanity of my mind that filtered my perceptions of life, I don't experience life the same way as before.

I have a lot more compassion for people. I'm not so quick to be right. I give people all the room they need to just be themselves. I don't judge people anymore. And what a relief it is to just let people be who they are, regardless of how they choose to live their life. Some people do try to annoy me, because there is something about them that makes me shake my head; but I just laugh and let them have their reality. This has given me a deep insight into my pre-Padre Pio life.

God, I can't believe how judgmental I was! I can't believe I was so conceited in my spiritual convictions! I can understand now why I chafed people. The truth is, now I feel much more relaxed with people; and it feels wonderful!

Anyway, Padre; I just wanted to let you know that *Healing with Padre Pio* should be out by next month, and I can't wait to hold a copy in my hands. I cannot thank you enough for what you have done for me; and I hope this book will have a healing effect on everyone who reads it. I know it will ruffle some feathers; but like you said, controversy is good because it causes dialogue, and the world could use a good dialogue on the Way.

If anything, I hope *Healing with Padre Pio* will help the reader become a little more aware of what the Way is, and that they don't have to go anywhere to find it; all they have to do is adopt a lifestyle that will awaken them to the Way—*because the Way is the Way is the Way...*

I remain,
Your faithful companion,
Orest

42. I'M BEING NUDGED AGAIN

Letter to Ascended Master
St. Padre Pio,
Saturday, March 10, 2012
7: 05 A. M.

Dear Padre,

I'm being nudged again…

For the past number of weeks I've been doing extensive research for my new book *The Summoning of Noman, The True Story of My Parallel Life.* My research started with C.G. Jung, who had an enormous influence on my life, and as I researched *the way of the dream* one window after another opened on the worldwide web of knowledge and I ended up buying books by Gregg Braden and Caroline Myss.

I had read Myss's book *Anatomy of the Spirit* years ago, but for some reason I had to reconnect with her work; so I purchased *Entering the Castle,* which is her work on St. Teresa of Avila, and *Sacred Contracts.* After I read these I will get her other books, because I love her connection with Divine Spirit and how she is giving expression to the Way through her own life path; and the same with Gregg Braden.

Braden has connected with his inner self and is giving expression to the Way by bringing science and spirituality together into a common perspective. I bought his books *The Isaiah Effect, The God Code, Fractal Time, The Spontaneous Healing of Belief,* and *Deep Truth.* I haven't picked up his book *The Divine Matrix* yet, but I have to because I know it will speak to my new book. I've read *The Isaiah Effect* and *Deep Truth* so far, and I found them both fascinating and paradigm-shifting.

I have to tell you Padre, I find it rather intriguing (if not amusing) that Caroline Myss should be singled out by one of your fellow Roman Catholic Saints to bring her divine vision of consciousness to the world. I haven't read St. Teresa's books yet (*The Way of Perfection, Interior Castle,* and her autobiography *The Life of Teresa of Avila),* but I plan to. Actually, Penny and I are going to Chapters in Barrie today to see if they have some of the books that I was nudged last night to buy, so I may see if they have any of St. Teresa's books. This brings me to the point of this letter—the nudge...

Since there is no such thing as coincidence, I know it was meant for me to go there, and by there I mean further research on Jung's psychology by way of James Hillman, who authored *The Soul's Code: In Search of Character and Calling*, and *Jung's Map of the Soul,* by Murray Stein. And I was also nudged to explore the poet David Whyte's work (*Crossing the Unknown Sea, Work as a Pilgrimage of Identity),* because he has connected with his inner self and is expressing the Way through poetry. If you will, his path is poetry, and I've been strongly nudged to read him so I can familiarize myself with his inspired language of the Way—because the Way speaks to us according to our own life path, and David Whyte's life path speaks the Way in one of life's most enduring languages, which is the language of poetry. In effect, by reading Whyte's poetry I will be "catching" the message of Divine Spirit as it is being given to the poet for today's world.

This speaks to Jesus' "directive" to *go with life and the living,* because that's where the new ideas can be found (he gave this advice to Glenda Green, who wrote the amazing book *Love Without End, Jesus speaks* that you recommended I read), and nothing can be more in the moment than poetry!

And as I researched David Whyte (who has one of the most magnificent poetry-reading voices I have ever heard, full, rich, and melodious) another window opened up to the artist Jerry Wennstrom who wrote the book *The Inspired Heart*—his incredible story of self-initiation into the deep mysteries of the Way!

During an extensive fast, Jerry Wennstrom was given the "directive" to get rid of all his art and personal belongings and live his life with complete trust in God's guidance. Out of this remarkable experience was born his book *The Inspired Heart*, which I have to read because it gives expression to the spiritual impasse that all seekers come to in their quest for spiritual self-realization consciousness. I can identify with Jerry Wennstrom, because I also "let go and let God" during one phase of my quest for my true self!

So, thank you for the nudge Padre. I will be ordering these books from Amazon, and I can't wait to get into them because I feel the call to get back to my new novel *The Summoning of Noman.* I had to put it aside while I edited *Healing with Padre Pio.* But that's done now, and I can jump right back into the River of God and swim with the flow of life and the living. Until the next time…

Your faithful companion,
Orest

43. PADRE, DID YOU PLANT THE SEED?

Letter to Ascended Master
St. Padre Pio,
Monday, March 27, 2012
6:35 A. M.

Dear Padre,

I have to ask, did you plant the seed for my next book of spiritual musings? Because yesterday the title of my new book of musings flashed across my mind: *The Riddle of the Good Samaritan, And Other Spiritual Musings.*

You told me in one of my spiritual healing sessions that my novel *Healing with Padre Pio* would end with a question, and to my great surprise that's exactly how it ended, with the very simple question **Why bother?**

This question was posed by Lorie, the woman who brings *Healing with Padre Pio* to closure. Oriano, my fictional self, tells Lorie that the conscious spiritual path of love is the most difficult path in the world to live, and she wanted to know why one would bother to live the conscious path of love if it was so difficult, and Oriano tells Lorie that her answer could be found in the riddle of the Good Samaritan.

So what is the riddle of the Good Samaritan? Why did he stop to help the injured man by the wayside when the priest and Levite walked by him? What was it about the Good Samaritan that made him show mercy on the injured man? In short, why did the Good Samaritan bother to help the injured man?

I picked Penny up at the bus terminal in Barrie yesterday. She flew in to Toronto from Thunder Bay where she went for her father's eight-eighth birthday, and she took the bus from Toronto to Barrie; but she told me that for some odd reason the bus drivers of both buses (she had to transfer buses in Newmarket) were not very friendly. When she told them that she had luggage that had to go in the bin, one driver gave her the look, which other customers noticed. One person said to Penny, "What's his problem?"

When Penny and I were talking about that this morning over coffee, I happened to remember that when I was sitting in the bus terminal in Barrie waiting for her bus to arrive I overheard a woman who was sitting across from me playing one of her Lotto scratch cards saying to a man who recognized her and asked what she was doing, she replied that she was waiting to catch a bus and then she said, "I hope I get a driver who smiles this time."

Why bother? That's the question that speaks to our relationship with life. Why bother to smile at your customers? Why bother to help your passenger put their bags in the storage bin? Why bother with anything if you don't have to?

Well Padre, that's the question I'm going to answer with my first musing of my third edition of spiritual musings, *Why Bother? The Riddle of the Good Samaritan.* And I know that the answer will come as a surprise to my readers—because, if I may extend the logic of my answer to its conclusion, one bothers because if he doesn't bother he will find himself in exactly the same situation over, and over, and over again until he decides to bother because that's the only way that he will ever break the cycle of his eternal return!

This is the riddle of the Good Samaritan—how to break the cycle of life and death, or karma and reincarnation, if you will. And this will be the theme of my third volume of spiritual musings—the secret of how to transcend one's life.

Okay, enough for now. Until the next time,

I remain,
Your faithful companion,
Orest

44. I'M BACK

Letters to Ascended Master
St. Padre Pio,
Friday, April 27, 2012
6: 50 A. M.

Dear Padre,

I'm back…

I just finished writing my new book, *Why Bother? The Riddle of the Good Samaritan.* I told you in my last letter (April 27, exactly one month ago) that it was going to be a book of spiritual musings; but my Muse had another agenda: it wanted to explore the theme of the three stages of evolution (the exoteric, mesoteric, and esoteric circles of life) using the Parable of the Good Samaritan as my entry point. Was that your doing, Padre?

Why Bother? is a little book, just under a hundred pages, but it's packed with the story of my quest for my true self; and yesterday I emailed two prominent writers (Jacob Needleman, Professor of Philosophy at San Francisco State University, and modern mystic Andrew Harvey) to see if they would endorse my book. I hope to hear from them. In fact, I asked you yesterday to intercede for me. I need your help because I really want to see this one out there. I know it has its own legs, but it could use a little help to get started.

I'm very proud of this little book, Padre. It's my way of paying Jesus back for all my years of holding a grudge at Christianity. Thank goodness you came into my life;

because hadn't you devastated my vanity I'd be still holding my grudge.

It doesn't matter that Christianity has morphed into the religion it has, because I now understand its greater purpose—which is for soul's GROWTH and UNDERSTANDING. I couldn't see this before you came into my life, but now I can. As you said, "There is more than one way." Just because it wasn't my way doesn't mean it can't be the way for someone else. I get that now, and I'm ever so thankful to you for helping me to see this!

This is what it means to not judge another person's path. Every person has to find their own path, and if one is content with their Christian path that's all that matters, because this is the path they need to grow in understanding. And when they have grown in all the understanding that they can with this path, they will move on to another path and another path until they find their way out of the cycle of karma and reincarnation.

Now I can get back to *The Summoning of Noman, The True Story of My Parallel Life.* I've been doing a lot of research for this book, and I've been keeping a dream journal—oh, by the way, thank you for the dream you gave Penny the other night. I know you were responsible for this dream, because it speaks to the symbols of the river and rock that you spoke to in *Healing with Padre Pio.* This dream helped Penny understand the transcripts of my sessions with you, which she was having trouble with. So, thank you again.

I may include her dream in *The Summoning of Noman* because it speaks to how the collective unconscious (Soul) speaks to the psyche to help one find their way through the spiritual impasses of their life. This is the function of dreams—to guide one though life's mazes; but I will be exploring this in *The Summoning of Noman.*

I have to order another ten or twelve books from Amazon for my research for this book. It seems that I'm waking up to something that I feel I should have been awakened to many years ago; but better late than never, right Padre?

And what am I waking up to? Well, it feels like I'm stepping out of the fog of my own vanity and I'm beginning to see life with much more clarity; that's the only way I can explain this awakening. And I know what it's leading to…

Okay, bye for now,

I remain,
Your faithful companion,
Orest

45. OUR NEIGHBOR'S YAPPY DOG

Letters to Ascended Master
St. Padre Pio,
Monday, May 21, 2012
6: 10 A. M.

Dear Padre,

Last weekend Penny and I visited some friends in Southern Ontario. They retired five years ago and built an impressive passive solar house in Colbourne. This area is apple growing country, and Penny and I would love to attend the apple festival in Brighton in the fall. In any event, we had a wonderful weekend.

Our friend Sara (not her real name) held a creative arts day Saturday afternoon. She invited members of our spiritual community to share their creative work, and a few members outside of our spiritual community showed their art work as well. I gave an impromptu talk on the creative process and read from my new book *Just Going With The Flow, And Other Spiritual Musings*.

Penny and I stayed over Saturday night at our friends' house, and Sunday morning we all went sightseeing; and then Penny and I took them out for lunch. It was Mother's Day, but we managed to find a table at a waterside restaurant in Brighton. We had a wonderful day, and I said to Penny that we have to do this more often; that is, make a weekend getaway and explore some of the little communities in Southern Ontario.

When we got back home Sunday night however we found our cat in a state of depression. She wouldn't eat, and is still eating very little. I wonder if she was traumatized by our being away for two days. We worry about her. She doesn't seem to be sick, only not eating and sleeping an awful lot. She was so sound asleep the other day that I had to pet her four or five times before she woke up. That scared me. I thought she was dead. I really think she was traumatized by our two day absence. I hope she comes out of it. We are giving her special attention, and she's only eating little nibbles.

Animals have emotions too, and I'm convinced that they pick up the energy of their owners. We have neighbors who bought the house across the street from us who have a little white Shitzu that yaps constantly. Our neighbors are a very unresolved couple, and they do a lot of arguing. I don't think they've spent one weekend up here that they haven't argued. One day I was sitting on the front deck reading and I heard them arguing and he said to her, "I can't wait till you die. I'm going to throw a big party and invite all our friends!"

One day they argued so loudly that they felt extra guilty and he came over later with a jar of homemade strawberry jam. They have two young daughters, about ten and twelve years old. He's a banking executive, and his wife has her own career. Yesterday I was sitting on the deck reading again, as I love to do (I feel so synchronized with my life when I'm doing what I love to do!) and I heard them arguing again. It was about their dog, which is always yapping. One of the girls yelled at her mother, "She's only your dog when you want to take her out for a walk! Can't you see our dog is psycho?"

I laughed, because I could see the truth of the girl's comment. I've known for a long time now that pets pick up their family's energy, and this family has a lot of unresolved issues. There's always an undercurrent of psychic tension just waiting to explode. This is why their little dog is so frenetic and constantly scurrying about and yapping non-stop. If it wasn't so amusing I'd find my neighbors very frustrating.

But they don't come up to their summer home very often. Their life in the city keeps them much too busy. One day though they will appreciate the quiet and solitude of their beautiful home in Georgian Bay, if they're still together that is. They probably will be, because they're Italian Canadians with old country values, and I just can't see them going their separate ways because they're bound by their Catholic faith to stick it out no matter what; but what a way to live, though. I hope they resolve some of their issues.

That's all for now, Padre…

I remain,
Your faithful companion,
Orest

46. OUR MYSTICAL CAT HU-LYNN

Letter to Ascended Master
St. Padre Pio,
Tuesday, July 10, 2012
8: 05 A. M

Dear Padre,

Our cat HU-Lynn passed away. Monday afternoon, June 25, 2012, I came home from work and went straight upstairs to check on her. She was dead, finally. She died in the left corner of my writing room next to my writing desk which she had made her own safe little nook. She had stopped eating the day Penny and I went to visit our friends in Colbourne, and for six weeks she lived on nothing but love and water; but she did not appear to suffer.

If she had shown any signs of suffering Penny and I would have taken her to the vet, but she didn't. Thank God, because we did not have the heart to put her down.

She just faded away with such grace that I can't help feel you had a hand in her passing. I wedged the little prayer card with your picture in between the baseboard and wall by her head, and placed a little stone that had the words BLESSINGS BE on it under your picture, and I know that you made her transition to the other side as gentle as possible; so thank you, Padre. It was a great comfort having your picture beside her when she died.

If you don't mind, Padre, I'd like to finish this letter tomorrow morning, or whenever. I picked up a little painting job and I have to go to work....

Friday, May 3, 2013

Padre, it's been ten months and I still cannot bring myself to finish my letter. In all honesty, I think my Muse would like to reserve what I have to say about our mystical cat for a short story; so if you don't mind, I think that's what I'm going to do. Thank you again for seeing her transition to the Other Side. She died in love.

Gratefully,
Your companion in Spirit,
Orest

47. BACK FROM THE DESERT

Letter to Ascended Master
St. Padre Pio,
Monday November 5, 2012
5: 30 A. M.

Dear Padre,

I feel like I've been out in the desert for a long time, and I want to come home now, back to the nourishing comfort of the Divine Current of God. Not that I was cut off from the creative consciousness of life; I suspended the flow and began to dry up. That's why I'm writing you again, because I have to re-establish my connection so the Holy Current can flow through me with the electrifying power of creativity that makes life worth living.

That's what happened to me, Padre; I began to lose my sense of meaning, and I don't mind telling you that I got scared. I've always been driven with purpose, but now that I have found the answers that I sought my whole life I let my creative muscles atrophy, and the result was a subtle possession by the spirit of futility—and God, do I hate the spirit of futility! It bores a hole into one's soul and fills it with meaninglessness!

I've been meaning to write you for some time now, but I kept putting it off for one reason or another. The last time I wrote you was five months ago, and I didn't even finish the letter. I wanted to tell you about our cat HU-Lynn that passed away. I said that I would get back to it the next morning, but here we are five months later and I still haven't finished that letter; but I will, because I have to share my feelings for HU-Lynn with you.

This morning I want to invite you into my daily life. I need your healing energy, because I've been worried lately that I may cross over without getting the books out that I want to get out. You told me I would be writing another book after *Healing with Padre Pio* based upon the research I was going to do, and I did start *The Summoning of Noman;* but I still have more research to do and I have been putting it off. I have to get my life back on track; that's why I'm writing you this letter.

I have to employ every trick that I know to re-establish my connection with the Divine Current of God. I've been doing a lot of research online and can't get over how many people have been opened up to the Divine Current and writing books like *The Word* and *I Am,* which speak to the *I Am Principle of Life.* But these books were channeled, and for some reason which I can't put my finger on yet I hesitate to read them; but I will order them and find out what they're all about. I've listened to the authors talking about their books, and now I have to read them to get the full story. In any event, the point I want to make is that I have to pull out the spigot so the Divine Current can flow freely once again in my life because I miss the energy of creative consciousness.

I have to tell you this, Padre. I've decided to change the title of my third book of spiritual musings. My title was *Stupidity is Not a Gift of God*, but I've had a shift in consciousness and find that title very disturbing now. It's in your face, and as clever as it may sound it's offensive because it lacks compassion. I don't know what I'm going to call my book now, but I think I have to get rid of that title—unless my Muse says otherwise, that it; and I am a servant of my Muse!

There's something else I want to tell you about my musings. I could write a spiritual musing at the drop of a hat, but not anymore. That's another reason why I have to re-establish my connection with the Divine Current of Life, and I hope that writing you this morning will begin the process because I hate this feeling of being out in the desert. It's dry and dusty and spiritually desiccating out there. I have to jump back into the creative current of life, and the best way to do that is to re-establish my connection with my own creative consciousness.

So, Padre; it seems I have the answer to the question I've been struggling to put into words this morning. My question was this: where do I go from here? And where I am to go, it seems, is back to the creative process. In short, I have to write something new, something that will tap me into the Divine Current; maybe my book *The Summoning of Noman*, which I've already started but have been putting off with the excuse that I have to do more research. What do you think?

Thanks for listening to me, Padre. I tried not to whine too much, but I had to get back in touch with you. I hope you understand…

I remain,
Your faithful companion,
Orest

48. THE NEW REGIMEN BEGINS

Letter to Ascended Master
St. Padre Pio,
Tuesday, November 6, 2012
7: 15 A. M.

Dear Padre,

I've embarked on a new regimen. I've strayed so far from the disciplines of my personal path that I have handicapped my sense of self-confidence. I've justified this spiritually desiccating period by blaming it on my health condition. My bypass surgery left me unable to do the kind of physical work I used to do; but I have to stop justifying myself and get on with my life by putting my best foot forward—hence, my new regimen.

When I was a long distance runner I could salvage the most rotten day by going for a seven mile run along the shoreline of Lake Helen in my hometown of Nipigon. It did not matter how rotten I felt or what kind of weather, by the end of my run I had salvaged the day; and by salvage I mean that I got out from under the burden of my day.

Well, Padre; lately I've been burdened by every day, and I don't like this feeling. It's so oppressive that I begin to lose hope; and hopelessness has never been my cup of tea. But this does give me some measure of insight into the life of people who suffer the despair of hopelessness. *"All we have is hope, but what hope is there?"* wrote the Canadian writer Margaret Atwood in a poem that I read years ago, which is why I've always had difficulty reading her books; they're clouded with a dystopian view on life, and that's too gloomy for me. But she's a masterful writer, and I commend her gift. So, what is my new regimen; and why did I embark on it this morning?

I've never been a half-measure type of person. Whenever I did something I jumped in with both feet or not do it at all. That attitude served me well most of my life, despite the heartaches that came with it (perhaps that's the karmic reason for my heart attack and bypass surgery); but I can't do that anymore. I have to take things slowly, with a measured step. This is why I began my new regimen this morning with a simple HU chant.

The HU chant (in my spiritual community we call it "the most beautiful love song to God") connects one with the Audible Life Current, or Divine Spirit if you will; and Divine Spirit being the creative consciousness of life, it's only natural that I would get back into doing my daily HU chants to tap into the creative consciousness of life. But what inspired me to begin this new regimen this morning?

I don't know if you planted the thought, Padre; but I woke up this morning with the realization that the new spirituality for the modern world has to be radically different from the spirituality of our past, because the spirituality of our past has brought the world to the brink of destruction, so obviously it's not working anymore. But what can possibly get mankind to step back from the brink of self-destruction?

The word "vibration" was on my mind this morning, and I couldn't shake it. And the more I thought about it, the more I saw that the new spirituality has to do with a gentle, practical way of changing our vibration to a higher frequency.

This is what all spirituality is supposed to do, change our vibration from a lower frequency to a higher frequency; but the old spiritualities of the world aren't working anymore. They have brought us this far, and they cannot take us the rest of the way to our true self; so humanity is in desperate need of a new spirituality that will raise the frequency of our personal vibrations which will automatically change our behavior.

This is why I decided to begin my new regimen with a morning HU chant. Penny and I suspended our evening HU chants, but I can't put it off any longer because it is the quickest and most efficient way that I know of to reconnect with the Holy Current of God—i.e., the creative life force that gives meaning to my life!

So, Padre; this morning instead of going straight to my computer to begin a fresh edit of my novel *Jesus Wears Dockers* (I've edited it several dozen times already), I decided to change my routine; so I read for half an hour or so (I was strongly nudged to reread Elaine Pagels book *Beyond Belief, The Secret Gospel of Thomas,* which I suspect is going to assist my next edit of *Jesus Wears Dockers*), and then I did a ten minute HU chant. And believe me when I tell you this, I honestly felt the healing energy of Divine Spirit flowing into my heart center where I directed it!

The reason I directed the healing energy of Divine Spirit to my heart center as I chanted HU was because last night I just happened to check out a book online called *The Heart's Code,* by Paul P. Pearsall (which I'm going to order); and I was directed to this book because of a You Tube video that I was watching on Bashar, the channeled entity who suggested to his audience that they read this book because the heart has a memory and communicates with every heart in the world.

Now, Padre; I don't doubt that you nudged me to watch that video on Bashar, who just happened to mention *The Heart's Code* that got me thinking about my own damaged heart and to do something about it, nor do I doubt that you planted that thought during the night that I woke up with, the thought of the new spirituality having to do with a simply way of raising the frequency of our vibration; hence the logic behind my decision to begin a new regimen of self-discipline, starting with a morning HU!

I KNOW you were working behind the scene, Padre. I asked you yesterday to come into my daily life because I needed your healing energy, and I KNOW that this is how you inspired the thought of a new regimen to get my life back on track; so, thank you!

So, starting with my simple HU chant every morning to reconnect with the creative life force (what in my spiritual community we call the Audible Life Current), I'm going to raise the frequency of my Soul vibration and align myself with the Divine Current of Life—the most efficient way to get back into sync with my own life!

And once I have raised my frequency enough, I know the other items of the list of my new regimen will come a lot easier; but I won't mention what they are at the moment. So; again I thank you, Padre. It didn't take you long to get back into my life; did it?

I remain,
Your faithful companion,
Orest

49. THE ANGRY SISTER

Letters to Ascended Master
St. Padre Pio,
Saturday, December 1, 2012
7: 05 A. M.

Dear Padre,

I have an interesting little coincidence I'd like to share with you. Of course, you know it's not a coincidence because you probably arranged for it to happen. By you I mean the omniscient guiding consciousness of Divine Spirit (you did tell me that you have the consciousness of all knowing and all seeing); which brings up an interesting point about one's individuality within the consciousness of Divine Spirit. So, if I may, let's clarify this puzzling concept before I relate my little story of the angry sister.

As you said, **life is a journey of the self**; but where does the self come from, and where is it going? And further still, what is the self? This has been my journey—to find an answer to these three questions. And I have found the answer. This is what my writing is all about—expanding and refining my answer with each book that I write.

The answer to these three questions is: 1, we come from God; 2, we return to God; and 3, we are Soul. But we are not conscious of our divine nature. This is what the journey through life is all about—becoming conscious of our spiritual self. And when we become one with our spiritual self we become one with Divine Spirit.

That's the short answer. The long answer makes up the complexity of life, because the journey to spiritual self-realization consciousness is an individual journey. As the Sufis say, "there are as many paths to God as there are souls." But if it's the same journey home to God, why are there so many paths?

This mystery took me the best part of my life to resolve; and the answer turns out to be astonishingly simple: because of our personal karma. No two people have the same karma. We may have similar karma, but it is never exactly the same; and it is the nature of our personal karma that is responsible for our karmic destiny, or personal path.

In effect, we inherit the life that we create with our personal karma. This of course presupposes reincarnation. One person is born a musical prodigy, and another is born mentally challenged. Both lives have been destined by personal karma.

But as I learned from my past-life regressions (which I wrote about in *Healing with Padre Pio*), we are pre-destined to become spiritually self-realized and God conscious. This is our spiritual DNA, and we just keep returning to life until we do.

We come into the world as sparks of divine consciousness, and our purpose in life is to evolve from one life to the next until we realize our spiritual purpose; but we grow and evolve according to our personal karma—which means that until we align our personal karmic destiny with our pre-scripted spiritual destiny we will always be at odds with ourselves; and this leads to the coincidence in my story of the angry sister.

Penny has a co-worker who was interested in my writing, so Penny gave her a copy of *Just Going with the Flow, And Other Spiritual Musings.* Jane (not her real name) read my book and thought that I could help her angry sister; so she called me.

Jane has two sisters, and one is very angry. She's been angry for many years. And this takes its toll on her sisters, especially their mother who has cancer. In fact, when their mother got diagnosed with cancer the angry sister revealed that she too had cancer; but this proved to be untrue. She just wanted some of that sympathy to go to her.

Jane's two sisters had come up from Toronto to visit their mother, and Jane called me to ask me if I could talk with her angry sister. Having read my book, she felt I had some kind of special wisdom that might help her angry sister; and I consented. After all, Padre; you did cure me of my deep-seated anger at Christianity, didn't you?

In any event, I knew that when it comes to situations like this I let Divine Spirit take the lead; so we arranged to meet at Tim Hortons coffee shop in Wasaga Beach. But on the day of our appointment, Jane called to tell me that her angry sister had changed her mind; but her other sister wanted to meet me and asked if I would bring some of my other books for her. She wanted to buy two of my books, and she let me choose which ones I felt would be best for her to read. I chose three, giving her the option of an extra one: *Healing with Padre Pio, Why Bother? The Riddle of the Good Samaritan,* and *Old Whore Life, Exploring the Shadow Side of Karma.* And that's when the coincidence happened.

On my fifteen minute drive to Wasaga to rendezvous with Jane and her sister, I glanced over at the three books sitting on my passenger seat; and as I looked at *Healing with Padre Pio* it came to me in a sudden flash of insight why Jane's angry sister had cancelled her appointment with me!

In the Prologue to *Healing with Padre Pio* I relate the anecdote of why the novelist Graham Greene cancelled his appointment with Padre Pio after waiting three years to see him. Greene went to Italy for his appointment; but before his appointment with the "living saint" who suffered the holy wounds of Jesus, Greene attended a Mass by Padre Pio; and he was so moved by Padre Pio's Mass that he cancelled his appointment. When asked by his friends back home in England why he cancelled his appointment after waiting three years to talk to Padre Pio, he replied that he felt the good priest would call him to a higher service; and he wasn't ready to do that just yet.

That's why Jane's angry sister cancelled her appointment with me; because she too felt she would be called to a higher service, and she wasn't ready yet to give up her anger. Realizing this, when I met Jane and her sister at the coffee shop I asked them to read the Prologue to *Healing with Padre Pio*. I didn't explain why I wanted them to read it; I wanted to see if they could discern why their angry sister had cancelled her appointment with me.

Jane didn't get it, but her sister was hit with a sudden realization and said, "Oh yes; that's it, isn't it?" And I replied, "You got it. That's why your sister didn't want to talk with me. She's not ready yet to give up her anger…"

And we talked for about an hour over coffee and the two sisters got some wonderful insights on how to best deal with their angry sister; but don't ask me what I said to them, because I got out of the way and let Soul speak to them.

So, thank you for being there Padre. I asked you to be present for our conversation, and I know you were. I do recall the gist of what I said to them, and it had to do with not letting their sister's anger control them. They should not give in to their sister and let her work her own way out of her anger consciousness.

"Tough love, you mean?" said Jane's sister.

"Exactly," I said. "Don't give in to her anger. If you do, she'll always have power over you and feed off your good nature. She has to work it out herself."

The sisters thanked me, and we went our separate ways. So there you have it, Padre; life is a journey of the self, and we can't make another person's journey for them. This is the merciful truth of our karmic path. What do you think?

I remain,
Your faithful companion,
Orest

50. LIFE IS A JOURNEY OF THE SELF

Letters to Ascended Master
St. Padre Pio,
Sunday, December 11, 2012
6: 15 A.M.

Dear Padre,

In *Love Without End, Jesus Speaks* by Glenda Green, a book I had not heard of and which you recommended that I read, Jesus tells Glenda to not be obsessed with figuring out life before living it; and he reminded her often *"to live, experience, and enjoy"* her life—which is exactly the same advice you gave to me. Remember?

You told me that I should live my life first and then write about it. You said that because I tried to figure out life I was getting in the way of living my life, and you wanted me to step back and experience my life; and then I could write about it.

And of course I argued with you. I stated my case that I was a writer and that it was my nature to think about life and write about it, but you insisted that I be fully present in the experience of my life first, and only then should I write about it.

Your logic was sound, because by immersing myself in the experience of my life I would be getting all the goodness of my experience—that precious "divine imminence" in every life experience that Jesus and I talked about in my novel *Jesus Wears Dockers*. Actually, it was not me who spoke with Jesus; it was my fictional self, whom I simply call "O" in my novel. But we both know that it was me, alter ego or not; and, believe me Padre, it was a wonderful experienced writing that novel!

In any event, I feel closure coming to my epistolary journey with you; and I feel it only fitting that I bring this little book of letters to closure with your comment that **"life is a journey of the self,"** because this is how we began our relationship, isn't it?

I gravitated to you because I believe that **life is an individual journey,** and despite the fact that you told me that you and I had made arrangements on the Other Side before we came into this world (you to become a Capuchin monk and me to become a writer), I had to be put through the mill of life before I could be pulled into your gravitational field; that's why the coincidences of meeting the woman who channeled you came about so we could fulfill our obligation to work together. But for what?

Obviously, as we came to conclude in my novel *Healing With Padre Pio,* to bring the two worldviews together into one worldview—the Christian worldview and the Gnostic worldview. Of course, Christianity will frown upon this because of Christianity's long antipathy for Gnosticism. But the time for grudges is long past. Which reminds me of a funny line I just heard on TV recently. Do you know what Irish Alzheimer's is? You forget everything but the grudges! That's what I think Christianity has—Irish Alzheimer's! It doesn't want to remember all the spiritual goodness of Gnosticism; and that's why you wanted me to publish my novel *Jesus Wears Dockers*; isn't it? Because in my novel Jesus and I reconcile the two worldviews!

Well Padre, I wrote my first letter to you on June 20, 2011, and I'm writing my fiftieth and closing letter this morning exactly one year and a half from my first letter; and I want to thank you for your patience, guidance, and compassionate understanding.

On the whole, our little journey has been very enlightening—even or perhaps because of the minor setbacks that I suffered; but I don't want to talk about those now. They're just too private to reveal, even to you!

How's that for irony? You, who have the consciousness of all knowing and all seeing, know everything about my life; that's why I have to thank you for your compassionate love and understanding. You know what, Padre? It just occurred to me that compassionate love is non-judgmental. Which means that **compassion is non-judgmental**. That's what you tried to get across to me throughout my whole spiritual healing experience, wasn't it?

In short, despite what I did that shamed me (although I learned from what I did and hope not to go there again), I felt absolutely no judgment from you. You just let me have my shameful way and learn my lesson, which I did. And you know what? I'm actually applying that non-judgmental attitude with people that bug the hell out of me, like certain movie actors for example. I watch them now with new eyes, and believe me what a wonderful feeling it is to appreciate them for their virtue instead of judging them for what I perceive to be their faults. Accepting the whole person, the good with the bad, that's what non-judgmental love is all about, isn't it?

But you did tell me that life is all about GROWTH and UNDERSTANDING. Well it's been quite a little journey, this epistolary adventure with you, and I really don't want to see it come to an end; but I have other books to write and get out—which I feel you very strongly nudging me to do. I especially appreciated your editorial guidance for my novel *Jesus Wears Dockers*. I asked you to watch over my shoulder as I did the final edits, and I know that your input made a difference because those little changes that I kept making not only made it read better, but they added to the integrity of the story; and that's what's most important to a writer—story integrity.

I was influenced in my youth by Hemingway's "one true sentence" principle, and I have tried to write everything with that aesthetic principle in mind; but that's another thought for another time. Suffice to say that parting is sweet sorrow, and it is time to bring *Letters to Padre Pio* (that's the title I've decided on) to closure.

I have two more letters to finish writing, but I wanted to write you my closing letter this morning because I just finished my final edit of *Jesus Wears Dockers,* and my journey with my fictional Jesus came to a sweet sorrow parting, and I wanted that same feeling for my epistolary closure with you; so thank you for your companionship, Padre; and I can't wait to talk with your again in our next project after I finish writing *The Summoning of Noman, The True Story of My Parallel Life.*

Ciao for now,
Orest

P.S. Penny had a dream last night of Nelson Mandela (who in real life has been in the hospital the last five days with pneumonia). He was in my hometown looking to get a copy of my book *Healing with Padre Pio*. I just thought I'd let you know that this great soul is reaching out to you, as if you didn't know!

———

ADDENDUM

A TIMELESS WISDOM

"Art is a process which goes best when the artist surrenders to random and unpredictable possibilities," Jesus told Glenda Green in her book *Love without End, Jesus Speaks*; which is what I do when I write my spiritual musings—and all the creative writing that I do, actually; like my little book *Why Bother? The Riddle of the Good Samaritan*.

I wanted to explore why one would be a Good Samaritan, so I abandoned to my creative writing process and got my personality out of the way and let Soul speak. Soul is who we are, our spiritual self if you will; and when I let Soul speak I have access to a timeless wisdom that offers me insights into life that I could never access with my mind alone. That's how I solved the riddle of the Good Samaritan.

The American artist Jerry Wennstrom came to the end of his creative painting process and "surrendered to random and unpredictable possibilities." He came to the disconcerting realization that his artistic process could take him no further on his journey to wholeness, and he abandoned his art and surrendered his life to the moment, trusting that the universe would provide for him; and for fifteen years he lived his life with total trust in the random and unpredictable moment, which he shared in his book *The Inspired Heart*.

"I trusted a higher good that I sensed was much better equipped to inform my choices than anything I had available in the limited range of will and intelligence," he wrote in the introduction to *The Inspired Heart*; and by trusting this inner guidance he reconnected with the spirit of his art and found his way again—just as the Canadian artist Robert Bateman found his way again when his artistic process brought him to a disconcerting halt. *"Is that all there is to art?"* he asked himself, as he studied his final abstract painting.

Nudged to take in a show of the American realist artist Andrew Wyeth's work in Buffalo, New York Robert Bateman studied Wyeth's work and had what he called his "road to Damascus" epiphany, and he shouted to himself, *"I found my way!"*

Robert Bateman abandoned abstract painting and went back to his roots, thereby reconnecting with his life's path in his new creative process of painting nature, which gave him all the spiritual succor that he could ask for on his journey to wholeness. Like Jerry Wennstrom, he had the courage to trust his inner guidance—that higher good that is much better equipped to guide us through life; but just what is this inner guidance?

The other night I was watching one of my favorite TV programs, *Recreating Eden*, a sumptuous gardening show that tells us as much about the gardener's life as it does about the creative process of gardening; and I was delighted to learn about the founders of the Findhorn Community in Northeastern Scotland.

I had known about the Findhorn Community for years and the incredible vegetables they grew there, but I had no knowledge of the founders of this community until I saw the episode on *Recreating Eden* that featured Dorothy Maclean, one of the three founding members of the community. I went on the Internet and did some research, and the story of how Eileen and Peter Caddy and Dorothy Maclean started the Findhorn Community was so fascinating that it took my breath away—because like Jerry Wennstrom, Robert Bateman, and every person in the world that has the courage to listen to their inner guidance, Eileen Caddy listened to her inner guidance and planted the seed that was to become the world-renowned model Ecovillage of the Findhorn Foundation Community.

Eileen and her husband Peter managed the Cluny Hill Hotel in the town of Forres in Northeastern Scotland, and after running it successfully for several years their employment was unexpectedly terminated. They had little money and didn't know what to do, but Eileen got guidance from **"the still small voice within"** to move with her husband and young sons to the nearby seaside village of Findhorn, and their friend Dorothy Maclean joined them.

"Findhorn started with the voice within; not just the garden. The garden came second," said Eileen Caddy; but why Findhorn?

The dry windswept sandy soil was far from being ideal for a vegetable garden, which Peter planted to help sustain his family; but because Peter listened to Dorothy's inner guidance on how to grow vegetables there, the garden grew to exceed everyone's expectations; and today the Findhorn Foundation Community is "dedicated to planetary service, co-creation with nature, and attunement to the divinity within all beings."

"I had an **inner knowing** that God was within and that I was part of a vast and loving universe," said Dorothy Maclean; and trusting this inner guidance that instructed her how to get the most out of their fledgling vegetable garden,

Peter followed her instructions and together they worked the garden and the magic of Findhorn began to manifest.

Dorothy Maclean had the gift of attuning herself with the essential intelligence of life, which communicated to her as nature spirits, or what she called devas; but however this inner guidance came to her she knew that it was God within, the **divine intelligence** that in my own spiritual journey I came to call the **omniscient guiding force of life,** the same inner intelligence that Jerry Wennstrom, Robert Bateman and all artists connect with when they are engaged in the creative process—but only some people take this divine intelligence to heart and live their whole life listening to the voice within.

That's how I wrote *Healing with Padre Pio*. The woman who channeled St. Padre Pio had an open house when she moved her spiritual healing practice from her home to a public building in the heart of the city which Penny and I attended, and she gave me a complimentary spiritual healing that excited my curiosity. The circumstances that led to my complimentary spiritual healing were so coincidental that I had to attribute them to providential design; but it was my choice to pursue my study of spiritual healing, and all because I was nudged by my inner guidance to resolve my deep seated anger issues with Christianity; hence, my novel *Healing with Padre Pio*!

Jesus admonished us to seek the kingdom of God first and all good things would follow, and he even tells us where to look for the kingdom of God: "When he was demanded of the Pharisees, when the kingdom of God should come, he answered them and said, *The kingdom of God cometh not with observation. Neither shall they say,*

Lo here! or, Lo there! for, behold, the kingdom of God is within you" (Luke 17: 20-21).

"Kingdom of God" is Christ's metaphor for what he called "the water of eternal life," which in Christ's lexicon is the Word of God, which is the Way; this is why I came to call the divine guidance within the omniscient guiding force of life—because it is the Way.

When Robert Bateman shouted *"I found my way!"* after studying Andrew Wyeth's work he reconnected with his divine guidance within and took his creative painting process to another level, which provided him with the spiritual nurture for wholeness that he was no longer getting painting abstract art. And Jerry Wenstrom. He reconnected with his creative painting process on another level after abandoning it like Robert Bateman. By listening to their inner guidance these artists reconnected with their inner self in a deeper, more meaningful way; as did Eileen and Peter Caddy and Dorothy Maclean.

What I learned from Jerry Wenstrom, Robert Bateman, and Eileen and Peter Caddy and Dorothy Maclean is that the divine guidance within will reconnect us with our life's path on a more meaningful level when we listen to that "still little voice within." But it takes courage to listen to that inner voice, as the poet Robert Frost immortalized for the world in his iconic poem *The Road Not Taken*. "Two roads diverged in a wood, and I—/I took the one less traveled by, /And that has made all the difference," said the poet.

One day we will all come to a fork in the road, because this is how life works; and we will be faced with the question to take the well traveled road or the road less traveled by. As Frost tells us, **the road less travelled by is**

our true life's path, which our inner guidance is always, always pointing out to us; and if we take it like Bateman, Wennstrom, and Eileen and Peter Caddy and Dorothy Maclean, it will make all the difference.

I know, because I came to a fork in the road when I was guided to pursue a spiritual healing with St. Padre Pio. I took the road less travelled by, and my experience with the Ascended Spiritual Master slew my vanity and healed my anger at Christianity and made me whole; and that has made all the difference in my life!

———

THE MAKING OF A NOVEL

JESUS WEARS DOCKERS,
THE GOSPEL CONSPIRACY STORY

Every novel has its own back story. Carl Jung said in the introduction to *Memories, Dreams, Reflections*, "A book of mine is a matter of fate. There is something unpredictable about the process of writing, and I cannot prescribe for myself any predetermined course. Thus this 'autobiography' is now taking a different direction quite different from what I had imagined in the beginning." My intensely autobiographical novel *Jesus Wears Dockers, The Gospel Conspiracy Story* was also a matter of fate. I did not choose to write it; it chose me. So what is the back story, then?

Jesus said to Glenda Green in her book *Love without End, Jesus Speaks*, "*There is no greater gift you can give to another than self-realization.*" This is why fate chose me to write *Jesus Wears Dockers*; because every novel blesses the reader with the gift of self-realization, and my novel's central theme is about self-realization consciousness. So my reader is doubly blessed—by a **conscious** and a **creative** intent.

When Francisco Goldman was asked by the *Paris Review* why he wrote his novel *Say Her Name* as a novel instead of a memoir because it was obviously the story of his passionate love for his young wife Aura Estrada and her tragic death by accidental drowning while surfing in the ocean on the Mexican coast, Goldman replied, "*I made things up in order to be able to tell the truth.*" Like

Goldman, I did likewise in order to be able to tell the truth about my life; but why I made things up the way I did is the back story to *Jesus Wears Dockers, The Gospel Conspiracy Story*.

I could begin the back story of my novel at any point in my life, because everything is connected; but I will begin with one of the most unbelievable experiences I ever had, and that would be my seven past-life regressions that I had when Penny and I moved to Georgian Bay.

Past-life regressions are so common today that there is nothing unbelievable about them anymore, but I had two past-life regressions that definitely fall into the category of unbelievable. 1: I was brought back to the Body of God where all Souls come from. I was an atom of God in the Body of God, but I did not have self-consciousness. I had Soul consciousness, but no self-consciousness; and 2: in the same regression I was brought back to my first primordial human life on Earth when I gave birth to my reflective self-consciousness.

These two regressions were the missing pieces to the puzzle of life that I had been looking for, because they gave me the answer to two of the most haunting questions that man has ever asked: *who am I?* And, *why am I?*

My regression to the Body of God told me that I was an atom of God, which I came to realize was a Soul seed that was planted on Earth to grow and evolve an individual identity; and my regression to my first primordial human life when I gave birth to my reflective self-consciousness told me that my purpose in life was to evolve in self-consciousness until I realized my divine nature, or Soul self.

But there's more to the back story. I had such an explosion of consciousness with my past-life regressions that I had to pour all of this energy into a new book, so I wrote my novel *Cathedral of My Past Lives*; but that wasn't enough to level me off. Then providence introduced me to the man who inspired my next novel, *The Waking Dream*; a water color artist whom I called Kevin Archer.

Kevin was in his late thirties, a ski instructor and sportswear salesman, and privately he painted; but like Robert Frost who was called by his inner voice to quit his job teaching school and sell his farm house in New Hampshire and move his young family to England and devote his life to writing poetry, so too did Kevin come to a fork in the road and was called to quit work, sell his house in Blue Mountain, and move to the "Hamptons of Ontario" and become a painter; but after a year of painting he hit such a dry spell that he began to wonder if he was on the right path, and that's when Providence intervened.

There's an old saying that when the student is ready the teacher appears, and it was destined that my protagonist Oriano Felicci in my novel become Kevin's teacher for the next stage of his journey. Oriano and Kevin connected in such a special way that all the gnostic wisdom of the Way that Oriano had garnered in his search for his true self poured out every time he and Kevin got together—*and many times it was purely by chance!*

It was magic watching the spigot to the "well of eternal life" open up whenever they were together, and the water of living truth just poured out of Oriano to quench Kevin's spiritual need to reconnect with his life's path in a deeper and more meaningful way; and then one day the following words poured out of Oriano's mouth and Kevin had the answer that he was looking for: *"Methodology will inspire, motivate, and cultivate the art process."* And every time they met thereafter he had new questions about his methodology, and he frantically took notes as Oriano and he conversed.

Whenever I write a novel I begin with a **conscious intent**, because essentially I am an idea writer; but once I begin my novel I abandon to the creative process and my story is directed by my Muse. Well, for whatever reason my Muse introduced Jesus into *The Waking Dream.* He made a cameo appearance in one chapter to firm up the theme of my novel, and the morning after I finished writing *The Waking Dream* I was still so charged with creative energy that I had to pour it somewhere, and I asked myself, *"What would happen if I had a dialogue with Jesus Christ?"*

For years I had toyed with the idea of writing a book about the secret meaning of Christ's sayings, which I had decoded; and after Jesus made his cameo appearance in *The Waking Dream* the idea struck me to write another novel with Jesus and me having a dialogue about the secret meaning of his sayings. And as always happens when my Muse grabs me by the "short hairs" with a new idea for a novel, I jumped right into my first chapter "Let the World Find Its Own Way," and I wrote with a feverish intensity every morning for three months before I went to work my trade until it was all out. That's how the first draft of *Jesus Wears Dockers* got to be written.

Writing the first draft gave me an insight into the creative process of writing that I had not realized: **a novel is a thought process that gives birth to its own truth**; and the truth that the first draft gave birth to was the astonishing truth of the "Gospel conspiracy." The phrase "Gospel conspiracy" did not appear in the first draft of my novel until the end of the book. Jesus mentions the Gospel conspiracy, and suddenly my whole story fell into place and the creative logic of the story made perfect sense to me; so I had to go back to the beginning and rewrite the whole book making the implicit theme of the Gospel conspiracy explicit, and it took a lot of weaving and many more drafts to write *Jesus Wears Dockers, The Gospel Conspiracy Story.*

———

AN INTERVIEW WITH THE AUTHOR

OPEN QUESTIONS AT A READING OF
HEALING WITH PADRE PIO

Q: Did you really speak with St. Padre Pio?

AUTHOR: I have to say yes. I can't prove this, of course; but I don't feel it's necessary to prove it, because life is an individual journey. There is only self-initiation into the mysteries of life, and my experience with the Ascended Master St. Padre Pio was an initiation into the deeper mysteries of the Way. Not only did he give me a spiritual healing, but he gave me information that puts a whole new light on karma and reincarnation. It was a very rewarding experience, and I can't wait to work with him on another book.

Q: Do you have a title for your next book with St. Padre Pio?

AUTHOR: Yes. *Padre Pio Speaks from Heaven.*

Q: Is it going to be fiction like *Healing with Padre Pio?*

AUTHOR: As I explained in the Prologue to *Healing with Padre Pio*, the story is fictional; but the transcripts of my talks with the Saint are real. The only changes I made to them were editorial, not content. I may use the same format with my new book, but I can't tell till I'm ready to start my project. My Muse will decide which way to go.

Q: Can you talk about your spiritual healing?

AUTHOR: There's not much more I can say that I haven't already said in the book. The most I can say is that it happened. I went into my spiritual healing sessions a very vain and spiritually conceited man, but I came out humbled. That was my healing.

Q: What do you mean humbled?

AUTHOR: We really have no idea how vain we are. After my spiritual healing I reread the *Book of Ecclesiastes*, and it made a whole lot more sense to me. I understood what the Preacher meant when he said that everything under the sun is vanity; but I don't want to expand upon that now, because I suspect that's what I'm going to be exploring in my new project with St. Padre Pio and I never like to talk about a book before writing it.

Q: How have Catholics reacted to your book?

AUTHOR: So far, with silence.

Q: I would think Catholics would object to your portrait of St. Padre Pio.

AUTHOR: If they do object, they've not shared it with me. It takes a lot of courage to put yourself out there, and people have to have deep convictions—not to mention a broad understanding of life—before they speak their mind. So far I've only received one review on Amazon for *Healing with Padre Pio*, and I couldn't have asked for a nicer review because my book did exactly what I hoped it would do for the reader; and that was to answer questions about Christianity that no one has been able to answer.

Q: It answered a lot of questions for me; but I still have trouble with channeling. I'm not comfortable with that yet. Maybe it's me, but I can't bring myself to trust it.

AUTHOR: There's only one way to prove it for yourself, and that is to experience it. I had absolutely no personal knowledge of channeling before my experience. I had read a few books by channeled spirits, the most notable being the Seth material, by Jane Roberts; but when I experienced St. Padre Pio in my spiritual healing sessions it didn't take me very long to realize that this was the real thing. Just the way he came across was proof enough for me. The energy was right, real, and very humbling. Besides, for dramatic effect I tested him by asking several questions in Italian. The woman who channeled him didn't speak Italian, and I didn't translate what I was asking; but St. Padre Pio answered my questions. That may not be proof enough for some people that he was real, but it is convincing. You also have to keep in mind that I didn't go into this just to get a book. I genuinely wanted to deal with my anger issues. I never expected to confront my own vanity in the process, because

I was too blind to see my own vanity; so it was a real bonus to deal with that.

Q: What do you think about Christianity now?

AUTHOR: It's a wonderful path for those that need it, but it is not the only path. That's the issue I had with Christianity. It believes itself to be the only path to salvation, but that's not true. That's what I had to clear up with St. Padre Pio.

Q: That's why I thought that some Christians would object to your book.

AUTHOR: So far they haven't. And if they do, I'd like to see how they justify that their path is the only path to salvation. That's on old song that won't play today. And if it does, it only reveals one's ignorance. Every path to salvation is valid.

Q: What do you mean by salvation?

AUTHOR: In this context, salvation means spiritual rebirth. *"Except a man be born again, he cannot see the kingdom of God,"* said Jesus. Salvation has many contexts; but whatever context, salvation is always about liberation. The housewife trapped in an abusive relationship wants salvation; the addict who wants to break his habit wants salvation; and the person trapped by economic circumstances wants salvation. The context may be different, but salvation is always about liberation; and liberation from life is the larger context that I have addressed in my novel *Healing with Padre Pio;* and especially in my follow-up book, *Letters to Padre Pio.*

Q: Which of your books is your favorite?

AUTHOR: I wish I could tell you. They're all very special to me. But if I were to single one out for you today, I think it would be *Why Bother? The Riddle of the Good Samaritan.*

Q: Why?

AUTHOR: I think because it reveals the secret of Christ's teaching. The difficulty with understanding Christ's teaching is that you have to live it to understand it, and the Parable of the Good Samaritan makes that point so obvious that only a sleeping soul would miss it.

Q: What are you working on now?

AUTHOR: I'm doing a lot of research for my novel *The Waking Dream,* but I think this is all prep work for the book I'm really looking forward to writing—*The Beauty of Suffering, Reflections on Jung's Red Book.* I can't wait to get into that. But I have to write *Padre Pio Speaks from Heaven* first, because I'm sure he will be giving me invaluable information for my Jung book. On the other hand, it's not really up to me which book I write. My Muse will tell me what book to work on next. She always does.

(Note: My Muse did tell me which book to write next: *The Summoning of Noman, The True Story of My Parallel Life,* which confirms what St. Padre Pio told me about living my same life over again. Apparently the first time I lived my life as Orest Stocco I did not achieve the outcome that I was born to achieve, so I returned to my same life to see if I could fulfill my Soul contract and break the cycle of karma and reincarnation; which, I'm happy to say, I did. And I thank St. Padre Pio for introducing me to the concept of parallel lives, as well as the concept of the karma-free life, which I'm researching for my next book.)

Q: Would you do another reading, please?

AUTHOR: Certainly…

———————

ABOUT THE AUTHOR

Orest Stocco was born in Panettieri, Calabria, Italy. He emigrated to Canada and studied philosophy at university. A student of Gurdjieff's teaching for many years which opened him up to the Way, his passion for writing inspired such innovative works as *Keeper of the Flame* and *Healing with Padre Pio*. He lives in Georgian Bay, Ontario with his life mate Penny Lynn Cates. His personal dictum is: *life is an individual journey.*

Visit him at: http://www.oreststocco.com

Spiritual Musings Blog:
http://www.spiritualmusingsbyoreststocco.blogspot.com

ME AND MY SISPYHEAN ROCK

www.ingramcontent.com/pod-product-compliance
Lightning Source LLC
Chambersburg PA
CBHW021051090426
42738CB00006B/289